The Myth of Self-Esteem
Finding Happiness
and Solving Problems in America

Contemporary Social Issues
George Ritzer, Series Editor

Contemporary Social Issues

Series Editor: George Ritzer, University of Maryland

The Myth of Self-Esteem
Finding Happiness
and Solving Problems in America

John P. Hewitt

University of Massachusetts, Amherst

St. Martin's Press
New York

Editor-in-chief: Steve Debow
Development editor: Anne Dempsey
Manager, publishing services: Emily Berleth
Senior editor, publishing services: Doug Bell
Senior production supervisor: Joe Ford
Project management: Publisher's Studio
Composition: Americomp
Cover design: Patricia McFadden
Cover photo: Copyright © Mike Jensen/Frozen Images

Library of Congress Catalog Card Number: 97-66312
Copyright © 1998 by St. Martin's Press, Inc.

Manufactured in the United States of America.
3 2 1 0 9
f e d c b

ISBN: 312-17556-6 (hardcover)   ISBN: 312-13715-X (softcover)

For information (Scholarly/Reference):   For information (College):
St. Martin's Press, Inc.   Worth Publishers, Inc.
175 Fifth Avenue   33 Irving Place
New York, NY 10010   New York, NY 10003
www.smpcollege.com   www.worthpublishers.com

For the newest member of my family,
Elijah Percy-Jerome Gardner

Contents

Foreword

As we move toward the close of the twentieth century, we confront a seemingly endless array of pressing social issues: crime, urban decay, inequality, ecological threats, rampant consumerism, war, AIDS, inadequate health care, national and personal debt, and many more. Although such problems are regularly dealt with in newspapers, magazines, and trade books and on radio and television, such popular treatment has severe limitations. By examining in these issues systematically through the lens of sociology, we can gain greater insight into them and be better able to deal with them. It is to this end that St. Martin's Press has created this series on contemporary social issues.

Each book in the series casts a new and distinctive light on a familiar social issue, while challenging the conventional view, which may obscure as much as it clarifies. Phenomena that seem disparate and unrelated are shown to have many commonalities and to reflect a major, but largely unrecognized, trend within the larger society. Or a systematic comparative investigation demonstrates the existence of social causes or consequences that are overlooked by other types of anlaysis. In uncovering such realities the books in this series are much more than intellectual exercises; they have powerful practical implications for our lives and for the structure of society.

At another level, this series fills a void in book publishing. There is certainly no shortage of academic titles, but those books tend to be introductory texts for undergraduates or advanced monographs for professional scholars. Missing are broadly accessible, issue-oriented books appropriate for all students (and for general readers). The books in this series occupy that niche somewhere between popular trade books and monographs. Like trade books, they deal with important and interesting social issues, are well written, and are as jargon free as possible. However, they are more rigorous than trade books in meeting academic standards for writing and research. Although they are not textbooks, they often explore topics covered in basic textbooks and therefore are easily integrated into the curriculum of sociology and other disciplines.

Each of the books in the St. Martin's series "Contemporary Social Issues" is a new and distinctive piece of work. I believe that students, serious general readers, and professors will all find the books to be informative, interesting, thought provoking, and exciting.

George Ritzer

Preface

T *he Myth of Self-Esteem* is an effort to describe, interpret, and criticize the contemporary American fascination with self-esteem. The book can be used in a variety of courses, including Social Psychology, Social Problems, Self and Society, American Culture, Social Theory, Sociological Theory, and Sociology of Knowledge, as well as Education courses.

Americans hear and use the word *self-esteem* a great deal these days. Magazines for parents provide advice about how to bolster the self-esteem of little Sally or Kevin and promise that if they are successful their child will lead a happier and more productive life. Television talk shows regularly feature guests who have been victimized by racism, sexual harassment, or physical abuse, and who proclaim that damage to their self-esteem is as painful as any physical harm they may have suffered. Many teachers fervently believe that the way to solve the country's educational problems is to build their students' self-esteem, for it is the lack of self-esteem, they hold, that interferes with learning. Hundreds of millions of dollars are spent each year on books, magazines, seminars, and audio and videotapes that are intended to teach people how to feel better about themselves and, therefore, be happier and more successful.

The rise of self-esteem to prominence in the American vocabulary poses a striking challenge to our understanding of ourselves. Where do such words originate? Why do they become so widely used? When people speak of self-esteem, what do they really mean? Do they even know what they mean? Have the proponents of self-esteem discovered a crucial fact about human nature, something that will cure our social ills and make our lives better? Or is the search for self-esteem, in reality, the pursuit of an illusion—a quest for something that does not really exist or whose potential is far less than it is advertised to be?

My interest in writing this book stems from my own sense of puzzlement that talk of self-esteem has become so widespread and from my ambivalence about this development. Although the word has been a part of our vocabulary for decades, if not centuries, and social scientists have long conceived and studied self-esteem, popular use of the term exploded in the early 1980s. Self-esteem became a widely accepted theory of education. The California legislature funded a task force whose purpose was to study self-esteem as a potential means of solving such pressing problems as addiction and delinquency. Popular theories of self-esteem were promulgated in advice books directed at managers, nurses, teachers, bankers, and other professionals, as well as the general public. Almost everybody, it seemed, learned to speak the language of self-esteem and came to believe that self-esteem is something worth pursuing and talking about. Why, I wondered?

Self-esteem is in several ways an appealing concept: Its proponents paint a cheerful portrait of individual potential that fits Americans' commonsense ideas about themselves and about human nature, one they claim is backed by mountains of scientific research. Most of us know people who walk under the cloud of a poor self-image and who seem to be their own worst enemies, unable to succeed at anything because they believe they cannot. And we know others who seem to take their own worth for granted, so full of confidence that nothing seems to stand in their way. It makes intuitive sense to attribute great powers to this personal quality, self-esteem, and to believe that if we could somehow foster self-esteem a great many personal troubles would vanish and social problems would be ameliorated.

The contemporary emphasis on self-esteem also can be irritating, and sometimes appalling. Self-esteem is now advanced as an explanation for every imaginable personal problem, and sometimes it seems one cannot turn on the television set or pick up a magazine without being confronted either with a victim claiming a loss of self-esteem or a psychologist offering advice about how to gain more. If only the insistent chorus of advice about self-esteem would stop and psychologists, and management experts, and teachers would find some other tune to sing! Moreover, the word seems to confirm our worst fears about the decline of ethics and morality, for people increasingly seem to use low self-esteem as an excuse for their every sin and shortcoming. Where even the vilest act can be explained away as an unfortunate but inevitable result of a poor self-image, our capacity to distinguish between good and evil seems to be in jeopardy. Moreover, victims of rape, incest, and other despicable acts often claim a loss of self-esteem. Why do people feel impelled to buttress their condemnation of wrongful acts with superfluous claims of lowered self-esteem? Doesn't such a preoccupation with psychic wounding undermine our capacity to tell the difference between right and wrong? Has the neutral language of psychology finally triumphed over the language of ethics or morality?

Self-esteem has all of the earmarks of a reigning cultural myth, a tale that informs us about what we should strive for, explains how to seek it, and warns us about the pitfalls that lie in wait for us. It is an unusual myth, to be sure, for it is not a story of ancient heroes and military triumphs but a contemporary tale in which men and women overcome mainly psychological obstacles to success and happiness. Its heroes are not soldiers but positive thinkers who lift themselves up by their psychic bootstraps; its priests and preachers are psychologists and therapists. Still, the myth of self-esteem functions much as any myth of heroic adventure or saintly miracles. It embodies and provides a language for discussing some of the key values of our culture, such as success and happiness. It provides a conventional wisdom with which to explain our own and others' conduct and to deal with life's difficulties. It is a source of inspiring stories of personal rebirth and deliverance and hope for the future. And just as heroic myths embellish the lives of historic figures, and even invent them when necessary, the myth of self-esteem decorates the bare facts of human psychology with ideas that are grounded in the needs of American culture and coated with the legitimacy of science.

In this book I will show how this myth functions in contemporary life. Self-esteem is a term of many uses. It not only is a word that Americans frequently use but also one about which they disagree. It is a word we use to underscore our belief that the individual is the center and measure of all things. At the same time, it is a word we use to describe the kind of treatment we feel people owe to one another. We sometimes speak of self-esteem when we really mean happiness or success, and our disagreements about how to attain self-esteem say something about the contradictory meanings that happiness and success hold for Americans. Self-esteem is our latest panacea, for social disorder as well as individual failure; yet, efforts to solve problems by enhancing self-esteem arouse heated opposition as well as enthusiastic support. In this myth of self-esteem, I believe, we have a profound mirror of our culture, a way of gaining some perspective on the way we think and act, and of discovering the contradictions—indeed, the problems—that are built into our view of ourselves and our world.

I am indebted to several people for their support in writing this book: Sabra Scribner and Ed Stanford, formerly at St. Martin's Press, who encouraged me to write it, and to George Ritzer, series editor; to Steve Debow and Anne Dempsey, who energetically and supportively saw the book through its final stages of publication; to my colleagues at the University of Massachusetts, who have been encouraging, and my graduate students in sociology, who have been particularly helpful—among the latter, I especially thank those who took my seminar in 1996 and 1997 and were exposed to some of the ideas in the book and gave me useful responses: Andrew Abel, Adrianne Bushey, Pat Duffy, Carter Gray, Phil Gullion, Karen Loeb, Jeff Lyons, Lisa Meidlinger, Jill Ross, Kathy Walker. And some of the ideas in Chapter 6 are drawn from my collaborative work on antidepressant drugs and the self, with Mike Fraser and L. B. Berger. I am also thankful to those individuals who reviewed my manuscript: Gary Alan Fine, University of Georgia; Viktor Gecas, Washington State University; and David Hopping, University of Illinois at Urbana-Champaign.

My self-esteem owes a great deal to my wonderful family: my parents, Anna and Jack Hewitt, who gave me the love on which it thrived; my mother-in-law Rose Livingston and my late father-in-law Jerry Livingston, who believed in me; my children, Elizabeth Hewitt and Gary Hewitt, who are the brightest stars in my universe, and their spouses, Jared Gardner and Madère Olivar, who shine right along with them; and my wife Myrna Livingston Hewitt, who is my buddy as well as my pillar of strength.

About the Author

John P. Hewitt is a professor of sociology at the University of Massachusetts at Amherst. He is the author of *Self and Society: A Symbolic Interactionist Social Psychology,* seventh edition (Boston: Allyn and Bacon, 1997) and the co-author (with Randall Stokes) of "Disclaimers" (*American Sociological Review,* 1975) and "Aligning Actions" (1976), as well as numerous other articles. He also wrote *Dilemmas of the American Self* (Philadelphia: Temple University Press, 1989) and was the recipient of the 1990 Charles Horton Cooley Award of the Society for the Study of Symbolic Interaction. He is fond of the Sonoran desert, Yellowstone geysers, western mountains, Bishop's Finger Ale, and a Labrador retriever, Spenser.

1

The Conventional Wisdom of Self-Esteem

idway through each semester in my undergraduate course in social psychology, I discuss the social sources and significance of self-esteem. When I come to that point, there is a visible quickening of student interest. Eyes that had been glazed by other topics brighten, and hands previously at rest are thrust into the air to ask questions and volunteer ideas. I sense not just an interest in the topic of self-esteem, but an identification with it, a feeling that I am now discussing something truly relevant. Students seem to recognize themselves and their peers in the ideas I present and the illustrations I use. Not just a handful react this way, for the great majority seem to be engrossed in this obviously riveting topic. I leave class with an exuberant, teacherly feeling that I have made a real connection with my students.

However, when in the next class session or two I begin to raise questions about the concept of self-esteem, students react differently. They are enthusiastic about the idea that self-esteem is something every human being wants and needs and that the quest for it explains much of what people do; but when I suggest that perhaps this is an ethnocentric idea, that members of other societies would think it strange to seek high self-esteem or to regard such a quest as part of human nature, their interest begins to wane. They listen politely and ask a few questions, but many seem skeptical and some clearly do not hear this part of my message. Confronted with the observation that some cultures expect humility rather than self-assertiveness, they respond by reaffirming their belief that the secret to success and happiness is to think well of oneself. I have begun to lose them, and I remember that this is what happened last semester, and the semester before that.

This loss of interest may be due partly to the complexity and counter-intuitive nature of the ideas on which my questions are based. The proposition that human beings want self-esteem seems simple and straightforward. The idea that culture may shape what seem to be universal human needs and impulses requires a more complex understanding of human behavior and a willingness to suspend belief in what seems so obviously a matter of "common sense." Students who are convinced that men and women have fundamentally different essences and who resist a more complex explanation of the cultural roots of gender can scarcely be faulted for clinging to the idea that it is human nature to want to like oneself. Perhaps it is simply easier to believe that one's disposition is genetically inscribed than to grapple with the vexing question of how culture creates a human nature, gendered or not, out of raw biological stuff.

There may be another explanation for student resistance. More than once it has occurred to me that in my role as a professor explaining the mysteries of self-esteem, I am more like a priest who is standing before an altar invoking sacred words that rekindle the faith of my student congregation than a social scientist who is dispassionately analyzing humankind. As long as I perform the rituals competently and sincerely, I reaffirm the faith and reassure the faithful. When I tell students that low self-esteem seems to make it difficult for a person to feel positive about others, and when I portray the downward spiral of self-regard that sometimes accompanies low self-esteem, I evoke nods of recognition and agreement. When I suggest that higher self-esteem and its accompanying positive mood is energizing and that it paves the way for accomplishment, I clearly strike a responsive chord of faith.

Just as Jewish congregants expect to hear the appropriate Torah portion read and interpreted or Christians to experience the miracle of the host, my students seem to want to hear familiar and reassuring words and to have their faith in the miracle of self-esteem renewed. Observant Jews do not want the rabbi to doubt the authenticity and importance of the text, nor do devout Roman Catholics want the priest to suggest that the wafer and wine are not the body and blood of Christ. Students' reactions to my challenge to their secular faith are less extreme than they might be if I were a rabbi or priest, for they know that professors of sociology are given to unorthodox views and expressions of skepticism. They do not so much seek to excommunicate me from the church of the faithful as to define me as irrelevant to it, since I am obviously not a member and not likely to become one.

The only students cheering me on when I express my doubts and reservations are those (fewer in number) who are themselves disposed to question this particular cultural orthodoxy. They leap at the possibility that what psychologists portray as universal human nature might in fact be merely another insupportable American belief. Yet their responses to the reservations I express also are discomforting, for they too seem to rise from deep springs of belief rather than from the careful consideration of fact and argument. These students seem as passionately committed to the idea that self-esteem is a cultural fabrication as the majority are to the idea that the pursuit of self-esteem is a universal preoccupation of human beings.

My students are not unique in their reactions, for a great many people with whom I have spoken about such issues tend to respond in much the same way. For the majority of contemporary Americans, self-esteem is an important and interesting topic to which they can easily relate and a word they can readily use. Few people have not at one time or another suffered blows to their self-regard and experienced the paralyzing effects of the thought that anything they attempt is likely to fail or that they themselves are worthless. Most people have at least occasionally experienced an almost euphoric feeling of self-confidence that liberates tremendous energies and leads to success in everything they attempt. Most people want to accept and respect themselves and are unhappy when they cannot do so. It is understandably difficult, therefore, to entertain the idea that human beings do not naturally want to preserve and enhance their self-esteem, and even though many people assert the value of humility, in practice, Americans are apt to hold the belief that one should like and be proud of oneself.

Moreover, just as some students express what may be a form of alienation from their culture by doubting one of its main tenets, so do others. As I will show later in this book, the passionate belief in the power of self-esteem is matched with equal fervor by the repulsion and dismay with which many critics of American culture greet its preoccupation with the self. Not everyone speaks reverently of self-esteem; some regard it as little more than narcissism, and they take it as their mission to combat this evil wherever they can. Their enthusiastic attack on self-esteem is likewise discomforting, for it too springs from faith rather than from considered judgment.

This divided reaction, with a majority of people expressing their faith in a major cultural term of reference and a minority of people expressing their alienation from it, is evidence that the word *self-esteem* touches a sensitive cultural nerve. The importance that is placed on self-liking or self-respect suggests that the idea of self-esteem is somehow deeply rooted in our cultural soil. The strong resistance to any critique of self-esteem or the expression of any doubts about the concept is evidence that when the importance of self-esteem is challenged, a major part of the contemporary American view of the world is challenged. The eagerness with which others doubt the validity of the concept of self-esteem also is an indication that this word and the reality to which it refers are as important to those who are alienated from American culture as to those who are committed to it. When we find people vehemently disagreeing about some aspect of their world, it is likely that we have found something of tremendous concern to them—people argue about things that are culturally important.

The object of this book is to unravel the assumptions that are built into the contemporary usage and understanding of the idea of self-esteem and to build a more complete picture of this phenomenon and the importance we attribute to it. To pursue this goal I must ask the reader to suspend his or her belief in self-esteem as an established scientific fact, to consider the possibility that it may not be as universal a quest as we imagine, and to entertain the idea that it may be something very different from what we ordinarily assume it to be. My purpose in making this request is not to persuade the reader that what psychologists and social psychologists say about self-esteem has no scientific validity, nor is it to convince the reader that none of the everyday beliefs about self-esteem are true. Rather, the reader should step back from this commonplace word and regard self-esteem for the time being not as a phenomenon that can be studied scientifically but as something in which people, including social scientists, believe. To learn something about the reality of self-esteem, we must first consider it as a myth—a set of beliefs contemporary people hold about themselves and their social world, stories they tell about themselves and their lives.

Beliefs about self-esteem are often (but by no means always) buttressed by science, and the stories frequently employ scientific theories and evidence. This is not to say that science confirms the myth of self-esteem, but only that it is enlisted in its support. The myth of self-esteem and the arguments raised against it go well beyond any evidence that science could possibly provide. Accordingly, in this book I will pay scant attention to the empirical studies of self-esteem conducted by sociologists and psychologists. Some of these studies support one or another aspect of the myth; many of them contradict the myth or reveal the sources and consequences of self-esteem to be far more complex than proponents (or opponents) of the myth would like to believe. My topic is the cultural and not the social scientific reality of self-esteem.[1]

To approach self-esteem as a myth, I will first describe a variety of ways in which contemporary people use the term. As we will see, people often refer to self-esteem. They use the word as they attempt to explain their own conduct or that of others. They insert the word liberally into their conversations. They devise techniques for raising their own self-esteem or the self-esteem of their children or friends. As I describe the various things people say and do in the name of self-esteem, I will raise a number of questions about what people mean when they use this word, why they use it in such situations, and why they do what they think will enhance it. After this excursion into some of the contemporary uses of self-esteem, I will return to the idea that self-esteem is a myth and further explore this metaphor.

HEALTHY BODIES, HEALTHY SELVES

A television exercise guru is performing her fitness routine before the camera, keeping time to generic background music.[2] As she jogs and stretches and jumps, she maintains a constant patter of commentary, explanation, and advice about fitness. The talk is of heart rates and target zones and the importance of diet. One imagines a home audience following her every move and taking her suggestions to heart as they jump and stretch and sweat. Suddenly, however, she is explaining that the aches and pains of everyday life seem to affect the self-esteem of men more than women. Men are less psychologically resilient to aching joints or injured knees and think less of themselves when they cannot do what they once could or would like to be able to do. Women lose less of their self-esteem and recover it more quickly in these circumstances, for they are not as defeated by failure, nor do they set impossibly high standards. Exercise and a fit body are important ways of maintaining self-esteem for many people—to keep self-esteem high, stay fit.

Self-esteem? As I listen, I wonder how the average viewer responds to this talk. I think of my own experiences in high school gym classes, where, had the word self-esteem been in my everyday vocabulary, I would have sworn the teacher's goal was to destroy as much of mine as he could by asking me to do things I was never meant to do. I speculate that perhaps the viewer has no response to the word, that such babble about self-esteem is drowned in the sweat and noise of physical effort, or that the word has become so commonplace that it can be safely uttered without transmitting anything meaningful. I wonder why the guru feels that the self-evident virtues of exercise must be justified in the language of self-esteem.

One way of questioning such references to self-esteem is by asking whether the message is really about self-esteem or, instead, about something else. It may be, for example, that the exercise guru is actually giving advice about the gender responsibilities of women. Be concerned with how your man feels about himself, the viewer is urged. Your strength as a woman gives you the capacity to maintain your pride under circumstances where a man might lose his. Moreover, your special responsibility and capability as a woman is to soothe a man's wounded pride and help uphold his self-respect. Be aware of his limitations, and remember that your job is to see to it that he thinks well of himself, even when he falls short of the mark.

If one looks at the use of the word self-esteem in this way, it would seem to be mainly a vehicle for expressing another set of meanings or ideas. Since Americans have come to believe that self-esteem is important, the fostering of self-esteem comes to be included in the responsibilities people have to one another. In this case, self-esteem is invoked to support the tenacious conventional view of the relationship between the sexes in which women are thought to possess the capacity and are expected to shoulder the responsibility for providing for the emotional needs of their men. Evidently, a woman's place is beside her man, bolstering his self-esteem.

Even if the guru's message has nothing to do with the responsibilities of gender, one has to ask why the concept of self-esteem is invoked. Exercise is good for people: it can increase heart and lung capacity, create a general feeling of well-being, and add years to one's life. Thus, self-esteem appears to be irrelevant, for if one can feel good by exercising, why is it important to point out that one can also feel good about oneself? Why should the exercise guru feel compelled to justify exercise by pointing out its effects on self-esteem?

One explanation might be that contemporary people often appeal to scientific facts to justify or rationalize what they do, thus they turn to the concept of self-esteem because it has some of the aura of science about it. Yet there is plenty of biological or medical science to cite in support of the value of exercise, so the fact that people cite and believe social science must indicate that something more is at stake. Perhaps it is not just the body that one is concerned with during exercise, but even more the self that one so carefully shapes and tones. To claim that exercise enhances self-esteem is to say that it is an activity that will allow one to make a desirable self-presentation.

SELF-ESTEEM AND PERSONAL SALVATION

A talented college student whose future had once seemed secure and promising before he began to use drugs is being interviewed on an evening network television news program.[3] After a period of involvement with drugs, he is now back on a positive track, and the story relates how he was able to recover. At a certain point in his life, he says, he found himself surrounded by others whose world seemed to be defined by an eternal quest to secure and use drugs. As he became drawn into their circle and began to use drugs himself, he was astonished to discover how rapidly he descended into what he would later regard as a hellish existence. At one moment he was a busy college student and at the next moment he was preoccupied with drugs and cared nothing about his studies, future, or previous circle of family and friends. He was lucky, he reports, that someone intervened in his life and that he received help in struggling to free himself of drugs and to recover his former life.

In explaining his descent into a life of drugs and his rescue from it, this young man several times referred to self-esteem. As he sank into the pit of drugs, his self-esteem fell ever lower. He would not have been able to win his battle against drugs without recovering his self-esteem, he says. He spoke of reaching a low point in his life and realizing that he would have to make the decision to change. He said self-esteem is necessary in this process, that he came to a point where he had enough self-esteem to be himself and not like the others with whom he had become associated. You have to like and respect who you are, he learned, in order to be what you want to be and to conquer the scourge of drug use.

Stories such as this one make a great deal of intuitive sense, both to those who have experienced a drug or alcohol problem and those who have dealt with the problems of others. Recovering addicts and alcoholics often learn to regard their former abuse of drugs as an abuse of themselves, and they recover their sense of pride or respect when they become sober or avoid the use of drugs. The friends or families of drug users or alcoholics often speak in similar terms: They see those they love destroying themselves and their lives and wish they could have enough concern or respect for themselves to stop their destructive behavior.

One's commonsense ideas about self-esteem make this word useful in understanding oneself and others. One cannot much like or respect oneself by engaging in behavior that others condemn, since self-esteem is rooted in the applause we receive from others for doing what is right, or at least from doing what they approve; and we intuitively grasp the motivational signifi-, cance of self-esteem—that people who like and respect and care for themselves are better able to do what is right and avoid doing what is wrong. Somehow self-esteem gives one the strength to overcome adversity and temptation.

Just as in the case of the exercise guru discussed earlier, one can raise questions about the use of the word self-esteem, not to challenge or support the theories on which it is based but to explore its meaning. When the college student speaks of the importance of self-esteem, he seems to attribute more than one meaning to the word. At one moment in his account, self-esteem appears to refer to self-respect; a person who can respect himself or herself has self-esteem. One way to regain self-respect and therefore self-esteem is to overcome the self-degradation of drug use. In this usage, self-esteem seems to be a result of one's actions; by abstaining, one raises self-esteem. At another moment, however, self-esteem is discussed as if it were the cause of those actions; that is, one can overcome temptation and self-degradation only by acquiring self-esteem. It is quite plausible, of course, for self-esteem to be both the cause and effect of action. In both the scientific and commonsense view, what one does is the basis for acquiring and maintaining self-esteem. But it is also self-esteem that provides the energy that allows one to act constructively and earn the approval and respect of others. As a result, self-esteem that is high or on the mend encourages behavior that further enhances one's self-esteem; self-esteem on the decline leads to behavior that further lowers one's self-esteem.

There is another meaning that lies implicit in the college student's talk of self-esteem. You can like or respect yourself, he implies, for who you really are instead of being what others want you to be. In this usage of the term, self-esteem seems to be based not merely or even primarily on socially acceptable behavior or the approval of others, but on following one's inner wishes or allowing oneself to flower in one's own way and not along the lines dictated by society. Each person has an essence, perhaps an inherently good self, this individual seems to say, and self-esteem consists of living up to that essence. This usage of self-esteem makes the word a synonym for self-actualization, for the pursuit of a self unfettered by the false expectations and judgments of others.

Is this young man merely confused about the nature of self-esteem and its place in his life? Is he unable to make up his mind as to whether self-esteem should come from within or from the judgments of others? And what is the source of this uncertainty? Is it a defect in his character or perhaps a confusion rooted in American culture and probably shared by many other people?

IT'S WHAT YOU TELL YOURSELF THAT COUNTS

A registered nurse writes in a professional publication, the *American Journal of Nursing*, explaining how her fellow nurses can learn to feel good about themselves.[4] She outlines a theory of self-esteem and suggests specific techniques for improving it. Poor self-esteem is an undesirable condition, she asserts, not only because it interferes with one's capacity to reach one's goals in life, but because it is inherently unhealthy. People should feel good about themselves. Follow her advice, she urges, and one's feelings of self-esteem will be enhanced.

Her techniques for helping people feel good about themselves are based on the theory that self-esteem ". . . is determined by the things we say to ourselves about ourselves."[5] Each of us has a set of beliefs about ourselves, and we maintain them in our unconscious minds by repeating them to ourselves. We believe we are intelligent or physically uncoordinated, and on various occasions we remind ourselves of what we think we are. Even if what we say about ourselves is not true, we tend to believe it because we so frequently repeat it. Much of our self-esteem is formed in childhood, and the beliefs we develop about ourselves tend to carry over into adulthood. Thus, it is possible to have low self-esteem as an adult, even if the ideas we acquired about ourselves as children are irrelevant to our present activities. Even if we are successful and well-regarded as adults, we can have low self-esteem because we tell ourselves what we learned to tell ourselves as children.

It is possible to improve self-esteem and to learn to feel good about ourselves, this author writes, precisely because our self-esteem reflects what we tell ourselves. People can learn to feel good about themselves by telling themselves good things. "If you bombard your unconscious mind with true statements about yourself," she writes, "before long they'll become the beliefs your mind will store and present—all to enhance your feelings of self-esteem." In other words, if we say good things about ourselves, we will then come to believe these statements, and believing them will make us feel good.

To begin improving self-esteem, nurses are advised to write down the things they say to themselves about themselves—the negative as well as the positive. "I am kind." "I am fair." "No one loves me." "I am stupid." Once the statements that refer to one's intrinsic worth as a person have been written down, the nurse on a quest for higher self-esteem should evaluate each of them through the eyes of someone who truly loves him or her. That is, the nurse should imagine herself or himself in the shoes of another, deciding which statements that loving other believes are true, which are false, and which are no longer valid, even if they once were true. The nurse should decide which of these beliefs are useful—that is, which ones encourage the pursuit of goals—and which ones do not. The nurse should, in effect, choose what he or she will believe and say. The object is to weed out negative and useless beliefs and retain positive and useful ones. As the author puts it, "Tidy up what you say to yourself." The mind is like a computer hard disk, and one should not corrupt it with "negative, untrue, or obsolete ideas."

Having performed this exercise, nurses should concentrate on telling themselves positive things about themselves. One way to do this is to write positive statements on three-by-five cards and then read them aloud several times a day. "I am a good person." "I can do anything I set my mind to do." "People like and respect me." Thus by talking to themselves in a positive way, nurses can convert these positive statements into beliefs that the mind will store and recall. They will feel better about themselves—and have higher self-esteem—because they will then automatically think positively rather than negatively about themselves.

As with the other illustrations used, the truth of such theories of self-esteem or the likely success of such techniques for enhancing it are not at issue here. There is some scientific basis for the idea that how one feels about oneself reflects what one says to oneself. One of the few successful psychotherapeutic treatments for depression (which is typically associated with low self-esteem), for example, is cognitive therapy. In this approach to treatment, the depressed person is taught more positive and effective ways of perceiving both external reality and himself or herself. People create realities by imagining them, and if they can make themselves feel badly by imagining the worst, presumably they can make themselves feel better by imagining good things. (Cognitive therapy is discussed at greater length in Chapters 3 and 6.) We also can make a case against the techniques this author recommends. The process of feeling better about oneself by asserting one's worth and goodness seems too easy and too simple. The human capacity to redefine reality only stretches so far, as most people have at least some negative experiences or qualities that cannot be so easily dismissed or imagined to be false!

The question to raise about this nurse's advice is not whether it is true or false—one can simply suspend judgment about that—but rather, how it uses the idea of self-esteem. What assumptions lie buried within her article? On what view of human beings and their social world is advice such as hers based?

The idea that one can feel better simply by giving oneself positive messages accords a great deal of power to the individual and downplays the significance of what others think. In much the same way as the recovering drug addict believes self-esteem is dependent on being "who you really are," the nurse/author believes that it lies within the capacity of each individual to decide what is true or false and then to lift himself or herself up by his or her psychic bootstraps. In either case, it is the individual who seems to be in charge of his or her destiny, and while others may play a helping role, in the end it is up to the individual to raise his or her self-esteem. The drug addict needed the concern and care of others, but in the end he had to decide what kind of person he would be. The nurse is encouraged to develop positive beliefs by imagining herself in the eyes of a supportive and loving other, but it is the nurse who makes the decisions about what to say and believe.

This approach to self-esteem thus implies that individuals can become relatively independent of the social worlds in which they live or that have formed them. Society—as represented by parents, employers, friends, or co-workers—may be the source of the ideas people have about themselves, but people can overcome these influences. They can put aside the false images they developed of themselves as children and replace them with positive images. They can decide whose opinions to take seriously and whose to reject, and thus decide which images of themselves are true and which are false. They can resist the negative things others say about them by giving themselves positive messages.

SOCIAL PSYCHOLOGISTS SAY . . .

A social psychologist is lecturing to college students about the sources of the images people form of themselves.[6] The professor attempts to answer some basic questions about the self: How do people come to think of themselves as intelligent or stupid, strong or weak? How do they develop positive or negative images of themselves? Indeed, how are they able to have any images of themselves?

The self, the professor explains, arises because we can imagine and adopt the attitudes others take toward us. In this process, generally known as role taking, we put ourselves in the shoes of the others with whom we interact, and we imagine how we appear to them and how they feel about us. We imagine that they think we are intelligent or stupid, or that they like or dislike us. In constructing an image and feeling about ourselves as we imagine it to exist in the minds of others, we also, to some extent, share that feeling. If we imagine that a significant other thinks we are intelligent, we feel we are intelligent. If we imagine that the other person is disgusted with us, we feel disgusted with ourselves. Sometimes we take these images and feelings to heart and become committed to them, thus acquiring self-images that mirror the imagined attitudes of others. Sometimes we are able to resist the imagined negative judgments of others and thus maintain a positive self-image, even in the face of criticism. And sometimes we find ourselves unable to believe the positive evaluations we receive from others and thus continue to think ill of ourselves, even in the face of contradictory evidence.

The professor goes on to explain in more detail the various ways in which we interpret the words and deeds of others and incorporate them into images of ourselves. Some evaluations and judgments are *direct,* for others tell us what they think of us in no uncertain terms: "You are a rotten child and I wish I never had you!" or, "I love you!" The recipient of such statements must engage in some role taking, if only to ascertain whether others really mean what they say, or are lying or perhaps speaking without thinking. But the statement itself leaves little room for interpretation. Other evaluations arise through a process known as *reflected appraisals,* in which others do or say something to which the individual attributes meaning. A student may raise his or her hand to ask a question in class, for example, but may find himself or herself ignored by the teacher. "This teacher never calls on me," the student thinks, "because he thinks I ask stupid questions. He must think I'm stupid." There may be a variety of reasons why the teacher never calls on this student, but what is significant for the student's self-image is the reason he or she attributes to the teacher's inattention.

The professor describes other ways in which we develop self-images. In *social comparison,* for example, we compare our abilities or possessions with those of others and feel good or bad depending upon how we fare. In *direct self-evaluations,* we come to conclusions about the worth of our own performances and develop feelings about ourselves—"I got an F on the examination! I must really be stupid!"—seemingly without referring to others and their standards. In both of these cases, however, the professor points out that there is more role taking than meets the eye. In both instances, the individual takes the perspective of the community or society as a whole in forming a self-image. "People who don't drive expensive cars are failures in this society," one may say, or "Anybody who couldn't pass that examination must be dumb."

Whatever its scientific validity, this social psychological account of self-esteem also is interesting for what it reveals about how the social psychologist views social reality. As a social psychologist, I think this portrayal is a useful way of analyzing not only the development of self-esteem but the whole experience of the self. In my eyes, therefore, it is "true" and "valid." But this scientific account is like the other illustrations I have used, for it too attributes a particular meaning to self-esteem and contains some assumptions about human beings and their relationship to society. Although I believe it more than I believe the others, I also think it is important to suspend belief in it so I can examine these meanings and assumptions. No theory or finding in social science is so perfectly formed or completely "true" or "valid" that it is immune from such questions. To put this another way, even social scientific theories and facts are closely linked to the culture in which they arise and to the ideas participants in that culture take for granted.

The most interesting feature of this social psychological account, viewed from this perspective, is how strongly it contrasts with the nurse's account of self-esteem. While the nurse/author seemed to view the individual as the final judge of what to believe and how to feel about himself or herself, the social psychologist seems to attribute this power to society. The views of others seem to count a great deal in shaping how individuals feel about themselves. Self-esteem arises because the individual imagines and to some extent comes to share the opinions and evaluations of others. Moreover, it is the standards of others—whether represented by the opinions of specific individuals or the general beliefs of society as a whole—that determine self-image. If one logically extends the aforementioned analysis, it seems people feel either good or bad about themselves depending on whether they do or do not live up to these standards and beliefs. While the nurse and recovering addict portray self-esteem as a matter of individual initiative or choice, the social psychologist portrays it as a product of social experience.

This contrast between one account of self-esteem and another is interesting because it extends a point made earlier. Many people, it seems, are ready to believe not only in the universal significance of self-esteem as a motivation but also in the power of the individual to improve self-esteem without help or intervention from others. Others not only believe self-esteem is important because our culture makes it important but also hold that the individual is significantly indebted to the social world for the self-esteem he or she enjoys. Those who believe in the former view tend to resist the arguments of those who advance the latter view. That is presumably why many of my students become restless when they hear me begin to raise doubts about self-esteem. Those who advance a view of self-esteem as something thoroughly dependent on the social world tend to poke fun at what they regard as the naive beliefs of those who think individuals can improve self-esteem on their own. Social psychologists who tend to take the former view become dispirited when they find it difficult to convince some of their students of its validity.

In short, the social psychologist seems motivated in part by a desire to argue with and overcome the beliefs of others about self-esteem. Although he or she might claim (and with some justification) that there is scientific evidence to support the social psychological explanation, there is probably a strong element of faith or belief at work. That is, the social psychologist believes a particular explanation not merely because there is evidence to support it, but also because he or she wants to believe it. And the professor trying to convince students of the social sources of self-esteem is doing so not merely because the evidence favors that interpretation, but because he or she is participating in a cultural debate, an argument about the relationship between the person and the society. The professor engages in that debate as a member of the society and as a participant in its culture, not simply as a social scientist.

FEELING GREAT AND MAKING MONEY

A management consultant is explaining to managers why they must pay attention to their employees' self-concepts.[7] There are, he points out, great differences in productivity between nations, factories, companies, and individuals. Some firms or individuals seem to accomplish almost anything they set out to accomplish, whereas others seem doomed to fail. The answer to the question of why these differences exist, the author says, is psychological, for "it is not latent talent and ability of people that makes the difference, but what is going on in their minds."[8] The key thing is self-concept, he argues, and the manager's job is to nurture it.

The self-concept, which includes self-esteem, is "the single most important discovery in psychology in this century."[9] It consists of the set of beliefs people hold about themselves, and it is a direct result of patterns laid down in infancy. Self-concept seems to determine everything—beliefs about the self influence how hard people will work, the risks they are willing to take, and how competently they will perform their tasks within an organization. "Even the amount of money a person earns is controlled by his or her self-concept," the author claims. "We never make much more or less than our self-concept barometer. . . . The way to increase your income is to raise your self-concept level of income and the external world changes to conform to it."[10]

The manager's task, in this view of the world, is to "create a task-focused environment where everybody feels great about themselves."[11] Organizations that successfully nurture self-ideals, self-images, and self-esteem are called "peak performance organizations." The manager's job in such organizations is really to help people feel valuable and respected within the company, like themselves, and thus encourage them to perform at their peak. The key to "peak performance management" is to help people feel like winners, for when they do they will act like winners, and the manager will not have to "supervise, monitor, or control them, nor lie awake at night grinding your teeth over the way things are going. You'll just have to get out of the way and they will perform in ways that will astonish you."

This management consultant expresses an optimistic view of the potential of self-esteem to solve human problems, in this case the problems organizations face in motivating workers to bring their best talents and energies to their jobs. This optimism takes two distinct forms. First, like others who emphasize self-esteem, this advisor paints a bright picture of the capacities and energies that are liberated when self-esteem is high. If a manager can help employees feel better about themselves, employees will do their utmost for the company and will need hardly any supervision; presumably the company's profits also will feel the effects of employees' improved self-concepts. Indeed, the power of a positive self-concept is so great that merely having one will improve an individual's earnings!

There also is optimism in the belief that managers have the capacity to shape and improve the self-concepts of those who work for them. Although in his analysis the consultant says that self-concept is laid down early in life—during infancy, in fact—he nonetheless attributes great power to managers. In their actions—and this consultant tells us almost nothing specific about what they should be—lies the future of the employee's self-concept. Thus, it is not only the individual who is responsible for his or her own self-esteem, since others—in this case managers, and later, as we shall see, teachers and parents—also bear some of the responsibility.

Beneath the surface of this optimistic view of the powers of self-esteem lie some contradictory, confusing meanings. First, although this management consultant attributes wonderful powers to individuals who "feel like winners," they nonetheless need help in improving their self-concepts. Evidently, they cannot raise themselves by their own bootstraps, but need managers who create favorable conditions for self-esteem. Second, this advice combines what seems in some ways to be a caring, humanistic approach to the individual in the corporation with a calculated effort to create conditions that will benefit the organization. The author speaks of the importance of people liking themselves and feeling valuable and respected, but the bottom line seems to be . . . the bottom line! And third, although this view of self-esteem is optimistic about the importance of self-esteem and the power of managers to improve it, there is a form of pessimism implicit in the discussion. If it is important to help employees gain their self-esteem, then there must be some forces that are working to lower their self-esteem. Perhaps the organization must work to improve self-esteem that was undermined by childhood experiences, or to repair self-concepts that were damaged by other companies. In any case, there seem to be social forces at work that lower the self-esteem the manager wants to raise.

HELPING CHILDREN FEEL GREAT ABOUT THEMSELVES

The comfortably middle-class parents of an elementary school-aged child turn to the pages of *Parent's Magazine* or a similar publication for advice about child-rearing. They do so not necessarily because they need specific help, but because like other contemporary American parents they have learned to seek advice from professionals—physicians or psychologists—that parents three generations ago would have sought from their own parents. From the 1950s through the 1970s, parents sought the advice of Dr. Benjamin Spock, who told them what to expect in the development of their infants and children, how to cope with their colds and cuts, and how to feed and discipline them. In the 1980s and 1990s, they turned to Dr. T. Barry Brazleton for similar advice. And then, as now, parents turn to a host of magazine articles by these and other experts to learn what children are like and how to help them grow.

The expert these parents meet in *Parent's Magazine* is advising them how they can help their child feel self-confident and resilient.[12] It is important for children to "feel great" about themselves, and according to the author, the findings of social science can help parents raise their children in ways that will produce such feelings. The child's self-esteem is always confronted with unavoidable "challenges and hurdles," its development continues throughout childhood, and its foundation changes as the child grows from infancy through adolescence. Nevertheless, early family experience is key to the child's well-being, and parents need to know how they can shape this experience in a positive way.

The key, says this author, is the "total or near total acceptance of children by their parents." Parents should distinguish carefully between the child and the child's behavior, always making sure to show love for and approval of the child even when his or her behavior is displeasing. Children deserve unconditional acceptance "for who they are instead of for what they do." Citing the research findings of psychologist Stanley Coopersmith,[13] the author argues that high self-esteem requires such acceptance. Parents should also, however, set clear limits and reasonable expectations for their children, and they should provide authoritative, not authoritarian, guidance. The goal is firm nurturing that will help build self-esteem.

Why is self-esteem important? The author's answer is eloquent:

> Self-esteem benefits its possessor and everyone who encounters her. Less critical of herself, the confident person is more generous toward others. Free from preoccupation with personal inadequacies, she has more energy and attention for what is happening in the world around her. Assured of her competence and power to make a difference, she can engage in efforts that are not limited by self-interest. In the words of Hillel, a Hebrew philosopher of the first century B.C.: "If I am not for myself, who will be for me? "And if I am only for myself, what am I?"[14]

The child who develops high self-esteem will be more creative, have the ability to resist social pressures to conform to the demands of others, function more effectively in life, and feel more satisfied. But more than that, the child also will be better able to accept others, capable of more satisfying intimacy with them, and willing to be interested in and concerned with people and activities beyond himself or herself.

On the surface, this author's analysis of the conditions that promote good self-images and the consequences of having them seems plausible and eminently reasonable. Like many other contemporary self-help advisors, she places a great deal of emphasis on the unconditional acceptance of the child by parents and others and, by implication, on the child's unconditional acceptance of himself or herself. Moreover, this emphasis on self-acceptance does not constitute a license for the child to do whatever he or she pleases. The child, like the parent, is supposed to learn the difference between the self and behavior, so the former can be accepted even when the latter is criticized. Parents are to give "firm nurturance" and set limits. The benefits of self-esteem established on this basis—creativity, concern for and generosity toward others, energy—likewise seem very sensible and desirable.

Yet there is a tension within this advice that could easily go unnoticed.

Self-acceptance is important, but so is acceptance of others. Children must learn to value themselves for "who" they are, but they also have the responsibility to help others do the same. Involvement and intimacy with others are desirable, but so is the capacity to resist social pressures to conform, such as children might encounter when their friends urge them to use drugs. Self-interest is inevitable, but transcending self-interest is also important. The child, in other words, must be self-interested and self-accepting, but also socially aware and engaged.

This seems like such good, commonsense advice that it is scarcely worth noting. The question here, of course, is not that it seems so sound to many of us, but rather *why* it seems that way. Does it seem like sensible advice because in scientific terms it is good advice, supported by the best scientific research? That is certainly the way this author wants us to view it; her advice is good because it is grounded in the truth of science. Or, in contrast, does the advice seem important and true because it resolves a dilemma parents—and perhaps many others—sometimes feel as they go about their lives? Our culture tells us that we are individuals, that we have a right to feel good about ourselves, and sometimes that even selfishness and self-absorption are natural human inclinations. In a society founded on capitalist "free enterprise," individuals feel entirely justified in "looking out for number one." At the same time, we hear opposing messages. We should be concerned with the welfare of our fellow human beings—the homeless, the ill, the oppressed. Self-interest is natural, but selfishness is wrong. Athletes should compete, but they also should be team players.

This advice to parents seems important and reasonable, I think, because it helps resolve this dilemma we sometimes feel. Parents want their children to be independent and assertive, but they also want them to stay within the limits they set. They want them to have friends and feel attached to others, but also to resist what they regard as harmful social pressures. And, perhaps, they want advice that will help them steer themselves and their children between these opposing inclinations—to be an individual, yet also to be a member of the group, to be responsive to the expectations and feelings of others, yet also to be capable of resisting pressures to conform and pursuing their own interests.

SELF-ESTEEM
THE OLD-FASHIONED WAY

An elementary school educator is writing a newspaper column in which he criticizes the emphasis contemporary educators place upon self-esteem as a means of improving students' capacity to learn and to succeed in school.[15]

He takes issue with a theory of self-esteem that he claims has taken hold in educational circles and now dominates teaching. In this theory, self-esteem is a precondition to learning, because a child who lacks self-esteem will be unable to absorb what the school has to offer and will likely become another educational failure. The remedy, according to this theory, is to teach self-esteem, much as the school teaches any other topic. That is, there should be time set aside to develop and bolster children's self-esteem. Teachers are encouraged to employ a variety of techniques to accomplish this task. Just as there are techniques for teaching reading or math, there are methods that will help children feel good about themselves.

This educator is appalled that schools are encouraging children to think that self-esteem is something they deserve to have, regardless of what they do. On the contrary, he argues, self-esteem is something that must be earned; it cannot be had on the cheap, but must stem from real accomplishments. "I've seen whole auditoriums," he writes, "full of students being told, indiscriminately, to feel good about themselves, being asked at random to stand up and give testimonials on how swell they are, and being reassured that by clinging to this confidence they will succeed mightily." The emphasis on giving children self-esteem, he argues, makes them think they have accomplished something when they have not, and it lowers educational standards, for children come to believe that whatever they are doing must be good enough.

This discussion of self-esteem is particularly interesting for two reasons. First, the writer attributes an effect to self-esteem that is the opposite of the consequences others whose views we have examined claim for it. In the conventional view, self-esteem provides a fountain of energy that enables the individual to accomplish great things. In this author's opinion, self-esteem makes people slacken their efforts, because if they too easily feel good about themselves then they have no incentive to strive to meet higher standards of accomplishment. The educational theory of self-esteem claims that children who like themselves will be motivated to learn and will, therefore, naturally do well on tests. The opposing view says there is no reason to study for the test if the child will get respect or approval regardless of how he or she does.

Second, this author distinguishes between unearned and earned self-esteem and links the former to unqualified self-approval and the latter to self-respect. Unearned self-esteem is gained without accomplishment and consists of what some critics of the self-esteem movement have called "feel-good" self-esteem. It is, these critics feel, a cheap imitation of the real thing, earned self-esteem, which is the self-respect people gain when they accomplish something of worth. Self-esteem is meaningless, in the eyes of such critics, unless the individual gets it the old-fashioned way—by earning it.

It is perhaps worth pointing out again that these conflicting views of self-esteem do not easily lend themselves to scientific tests of their validity, nor is empirical evidence the standard that opponents want to apply. Those who believe self-esteem is an unqualified right are not likely to be swayed by any evidence that "unearned" self-esteem is problematic. Those who believe self-esteem is valid only if earned are unlikely to be affected by evidence that self-esteem must rest upon the child's secure sense of unqualified love and acceptance. Nor is scientific evidence really relevant here, since our interest is in what the members of a society believe and not whether we can confirm or disconfirm it by scientific means.

THE NATURE OF MYTHS

Each of the foregoing vignettes describes a social setting in which the concept of self-esteem figures in the way people conceive of solutions to their problems, explain their successes or failures, or advise others on how to improve their lives. The word self-esteem is used in a variety of ways, sometimes in surprising contexts, and with meanings that oftentimes are at odds with one another. The task now is to begin to make some sense of the various and sometimes conflicting meanings of self-esteem. To do this, I must return to my premise that self-esteem is a myth.

It may seem peculiar for a practicing social psychologist (species sociologicus) to treat self-esteem as a myth. In common usage, to refer to an idea or a story as a myth is to consider it false or fictitious and to regard those who believe in it as naive or uncritical. Adults, for example, take a strange delight in convincing their gullible young children that a mythical person named Santa Claus actually climbs down the chimneys of all the good little boys and girls in the world during his yearly journey on Christmas Eve. The word *myth* also sometimes carries the connotation of *ideology*—that is, a set of widely accepted ideas and beliefs that justify or reinforce existing customs or social arrangements. The false idea that black people are morally or intellectually inferior to white people, for example, was used to justify the institution of slavery, and even today some people use it to justify the unequal treatment of African Americans or to explain why they are disadvantaged compared with other groups. How can I treat one of the core ideas of social psychology as if it were mere fiction or ideology?

Even the more restricted meaning of myth as a traditional story about the heroism of ancestors, the doings of supernatural beings, or the creation of the world does not seem to fit self-esteem. The concept of self-esteem is one of relatively recent origin, and it has been developed and elaborated on primarily by social scientists and by those, such as educators or therapists, who make use of their findings. There is little that is ancient about self-esteem, and those whose stories of recovery from addiction or rise to success emphasize self-esteem scarcely seem heroic in the traditional sense.

Tales of self-esteem seem to focus on the creation or recreation of the self, not of the world. How, then, is self-esteem a myth?

The answer to these questions is that myth provides a useful metaphor that helps one understand how ideas about self-esteem are employed by various people in contemporary American society. Whatever the scientific status of the concept—and the reader will recall that we have decided to put that question aside—its widespread usage has many of the earmarks of mythology. Like any metaphor, the treatment of self-esteem as a myth only takes one so far, and at some point it becomes more of a hindrance than a help and so must be abandoned. But up to that point, the metaphor helps one see aspects of self-esteem that we would otherwise overlook.

First, myths tell stories of various kinds. They narrate the accomplishments, exploits, and tribulations of real or fictitious individuals who embody the values or ideals of a particular culture. The biblical story of Job, for example, narrates the life of a man whose belief in God is put to the test through a series of misfortunes inflicted by that very God. Job is prosperous as well as upright and God-fearing, and Satan virtually dares God to inflict harm upon him, arguing that when he does, Job will no longer be so faithful or upright. Job's livestock are stolen, his servants and sons and daughters are killed, and finally his body is covered with boils from head to foot. At first, he holds steadfast to the idea that he should be prepared to accept God's will, but finally Job's patience is exhausted and he curses the day he was born and enters into a long and bitter argument with his friends and then with God himself. At last he acknowledges God's omnipotence and repents his blasphemy. God rewards his uprightness and belief lavishly, and Job becomes even more prosperous than he was and lives another 140 years.

The stories of individuals who recover self-esteem and climb out of the pit of addiction scarcely seem biblical in scope or significance. Job, after all, is part of the shared culture of a good part of the Western world, of Christians as well as Jews. His story is widely known and repeated, the topic of sermons and a template for derivative stories, such as the 1958 play *JB* by Archibald MacLeish in which a contemporary individual struggles with similar difficulties. The typical story of self-esteem bootstrapping, in contrast, is one told by an ordinary person, disseminated in the mass media rather than enshrined in a sacred book and told in the lame prose of psychology rather than in striking biblical images.

Yet like the story of Job, the inspiring stories of people who gain self-esteem and make their lives right manifest the key beliefs of a culture. In the Bible, it is Job's restored belief in the absolute power of God that constitutes his virtue. In modern tales of self-esteem, it is the recovery of belief in the unlimited powers of the individual that is valued. In either case, the myth tells the story of people who in the end become what their culture urges them to be.

Second, myths reveal or embody what we can call a culture's "ethno-psychology."[16] Every culture contains a set of ideas and beliefs about the nature of human beings, what motivates them to act, the way they perceive the world, how their minds work, and the emotions that are natural to them. Cultures differ, sometimes in profound ways, in their beliefs about the psychology of human beings. For example, while Americans believe people make rational choices and do what will most benefit them, other cultures may expect people to be motivated primarily by their loyalty to kin or their allegiance to a particular deity. While Americans may think that an emotion they call "grief" is the natural response to the death of a loved one, others may believe it is natural to feel "ill" in that situation.[17] While members of one culture may think men are sexually aggressive and women are reticent, members of another culture may hold the exact opposite view.

The ethnopsychology of contemporary American culture is strongly influenced, though not completely shaped, by the social sciences, particularly by the discipline of psychology. That is, Americans tend to turn to psychological theories and research to tell them about the nature of human thought, feeling, and action, although they are probably most likely to accept those ideas and findings that agree with what they already believe. When confronted with a troublesome event, such as the tragic deaths of several students in an automobile accident, high school officials call in psychologists to provide therapy for fellow students. When faced with an epidemic of drug abuse, Americans are apt to look to psychological theories in their search for solutions to the problem.

Because American ethnopsychology is heavily influenced by academic psychology, our myths tend to be permeated with psychological ideas and concepts.[18] As a result, myths such as the story of Job tend to be far less believable or even intelligible to Americans than myths that stress the individual's capacity to recover self-regard and fight an uphill but eventually successful battle against addiction, poverty, or some other undesirable condition. The story of Job makes sense to those whose ethnopsychology stresses the subservience of human beings to God. They take it for granted that what Job must do is submit to God rather than argue or curse. Although they see Job as capable of blasphemy, in their view he reveals his better self when he chooses to be steadfast in his faith. Few contemporary Americans hold such a view of human nature, for they believe human beings should be proud rather than humble; thus they are far more likely to believe myths in which the individual accomplishes something—whether it is the individual whose self-esteem makes it possible to conquer adversity or whose tremendous physical size and strength, like that of John Henry or Paul Bunyan (or perhaps nowadays Arnold Schwarzenegger), makes possible amazing feats.

Third, myths explain and justify social reality. It is not difficult to see how the story of Job functions in this way, for it counsels religious faith and patience in the face of adversity. Those who suffer setbacks or deprivation are encouraged to accept their lot as God's will, and thus to submit to it rather than to battle their circumstances. Naturally, this belief nicely serves the interests of those who currently benefit from the way society's benefits are distributed. Likewise, the myth that women are especially endowed as guardians of morality and custodians of the household, which was constructed largely during the nineteenth century, serves the interests of men in keeping women "in their place." The confinement of women to the domestic sphere was justified by the myth that men and women were naturally fitted to inhabit and control "separate spheres," one public, the other private.

Psychological myths explain and justify social reality by attributing problems to individuals rather than to the social world. The belief that individuals can improve their chances in life by improving their self-esteem seems to be, in one sense, a doctrine that celebrates the power of the individual. If not exactly heroic, the individual nonetheless possesses considerable power to shape his or her fate through sheer self-affirmation and self-confidence. But this myth of self-esteem also assigns great responsibility to the individual, for it says, in effect, that only the individual can be responsible for his or her situation. It is the individual who must recover self-esteem and thereby overcome adversity; and if the individual fails to do this, he or she is to blame. The possible influence of the social world is simply left out of the picture.

Finally, myths attempt to bridge disputes and assuage anxieties, for every culture contains some matters about which people disagree or with which they seem inordinately preoccupied. Social scientists customarily define culture as the knowledge, norms, and values shared by the members of a society. Thus, ideas about differences between men and women or about behavior considered inappropriate for children or about the ultimate purpose of human existence are all a part of culture. This emphasis on shared outlooks can obscure an important feature of culture, namely that the members of a society also share anxieties or worries about truth, disputes about norms, and ongoing arguments about values. Culture does not seem to provide people with a flawless and smoothly functioning guidance system for their individual and collective lives, but often subjects them to conflicting norms and values and, far from reassuring them about the meaning of life, makes them worry about it.

We can see hints of the disputes and anxieties that trouble Americans in the vignettes previously examined. The recovering addict, for example, links self-esteem to one's capacity to accept oneself for what one truly is (whatever that may be), for one can have self-esteem only to the extent one achieves self-acceptance. One does not have to attain self-esteem by doing anything that others value or reward, but only by accepting oneself for what one is. The management consultant, in contrast, seems to link self-esteem to accomplishment, since the manager's job is to help people like and respect themselves so they will perform better. It is the "peak performance" that validates not only the manager's efforts but also the employee's self-esteem.

These vignettes suggest that Americans may be tempted by two different and rather contradictory ways of attaining self-esteem. One way requires the individual to accomplish something—to achieve a socially valued goal such as success in climbing the corporate ladder—to attain self-esteem. The other way simply requires self-acceptance, for one is, in this view, entitled to feel good about oneself, regardless of one's accomplishments, just by being "who one really is." Myths of self-esteem reveal these differing routes to self-esteem, but they also attempt to deal with anxieties regarding which route to take. Stories about people who find happiness and self-esteem by accepting who they are reassure those who have chosen this route that they are behaving in an honorable and culturally appropriate way. They also provide images of an alternative way of life for those who feel anxious about their capacity to achieve self-esteem by succeeding in business or in some other competitive endeavor. Such myths also attempt to reconcile cultural contradictions or disputes. The management consultant's advice, for example, can be read as an attempt to reconcile our culture's emphasis on unconditional self-liking with its tendency to base self-worth on accomplishment.

In the following chapters I will explore the forms and varieties of the myth of self-esteem. I will examine its stories, see how it reveals American ethnopsychology, show how it explains and justifies social reality, and explore the cultural tensions it reveals. An appropriate starting point for this effort is an account of the social and cultural foundations of the concept of self-esteem. The word and the ideas it evokes have deep roots in American cultural soil. After examining the cultural roots of contemporary ideas about self-esteem in Chapter 2, I will turn in Chapter 3 to a discussion of the conceptual entrepreneurs who have made self-esteem a household word. Chapter 4 will examine the widespread use of self-esteem theory in education and will begin to develop a sociological interpretation of its appeal. Chapter 5 will examine the diverse meanings of self-esteem and relate them to features of American culture. And Chapter 6 will turn from the myth of self-esteem to an alternative way of viewing this phenomenon.

NOTES

1. Readers interested in the sociological and psychological literature on self-esteem can consult a number of authoritative sources. See, for

example, Morris Rosenberg, *Conceiving the Self* (New York: Basic Books, 1979); Morris Rosenberg and Roberta G. Simmons, *Black and White Self-Esteem: The Urban School Child* (Washington, D. C.: American Sociological Association, 1972); L. Edward Wells and Gerald Marwell, *Self-Esteem* (Beverly Hills: Sage, 1976); Ruth Wylie, *The Self-Concept: Theory and Research on Selected Topics* (Lincoln: University of Nebraska Press, 1979); Andrew M. Mecca, Neil J. Smelser, and John Vasconcellos, eds., *The Social Importance of Self-Esteem* (Berkeley: University of California Press, 1989); and Viktor Gecas and Peter Burke, "Self and Identity," Chapter 2 in Karen Cook, Gary Alan Fine, and James S. House, *Sociological Perspectives on Social Psychology* (Boston: Allyn and Bacon, 1995).

2. The description of the fitness guru is a composite of several such individuals; the reference to self-esteem actually occurred.
3. *CBS Evening News with Dan Rather,* Spring 1995, exact date uncertain.
4. Ruth D. Grainger, "How to Feel Good about Being You," *American Journal of Nursing* 90, April 1990: 14.
5. All material quoted in this and the following paragraph is from Grainger, p. 14.
6. The social psychologist is an imaginary, but representative, sociological social psychologist.
7. Brian Tracey, "I Can't, I Can't: How Self-Concept Shapes Performance," *Management World* 15, April–May, 1986: 1, 8.
8. Ibid.
9. Ibid.
10. Ibid., 8.
11. Quotations in this paragraph, ibid.
12. Anne C. Bernstein, "Feeling Great (About Myself): How Can You Help Your Child Feel Self-confident and Resilient?" *Parents' Magazine* 57, September 1982: 51–56.
13. Stanley Coopersmith, *The Antecedents of Self-Esteem.* San Francisco: W. H. Freeman, 1967.
14. Ibid., 56. Hillel's saying actually includes an additional question: "And if not now, when?"
15. Mike Schmoker, "Self-Esteem is Earned, Not Learned." *Los Angeles Times* 108, October 7, 1989: Sect. 2, p. 8.
16. For useful articles on the concept of ethnopsychology, see Theodore Schwartz, Geoffrey M. White, and Catherine A. Lutz, eds. *New Directions in Psychological Anthropology* (New York: Cambridge University Press, 1992). Also see Richard A. Schweder and Robert A. LeVine, eds., *Culture Theory: Essays on Mind, Self, and Emotion* (New York: Cambridge University Press, 1984).

17. See, for example, Robert I. Levy, *The Tahitians*. Chicago: University of Chicago Press, 1973.
18. American ethnopsychology also strongly influences psychology and social psychology. For a discussion of ethnocentrism in social psychology, see Hazel R. Markus and S. Kitayama, "Culture and the Self: Implications for Cognition, Emotion, and Motivation." *Psychological Review* 98, 1991: 224–253.

2

Creating the Language of Self

To examine self-esteem as a myth we must look at it in the same way we would look at any myth. We must examine its cultural roots, discover who promotes the myth, and consider why people believe in it. The stories human beings repeat do not miraculously spring into their minds. Someone once told the stories, and although we can seldom trace them to their ultimate creators, we can understand them better if we know something about their genealogy. Myths do not remain static, but change and grow over time, so what we now consider the truth was once a different truth. And behind myths lie needs and interests, for human beings have a purpose in passing on their stories to new generations. They seek to reassure themselves or relieve anxieties, to explain the good or bad things that happen to them, and sometimes to maintain their influence and power.

In this chapter I will examine the social and cultural basis of the myth of self-esteem. A full-scale social history of self-esteem would require a book much larger than this one. But it is important to understand that this very current word is not new. It has been used for at least a century with something like its contemporary range of meanings in the United States. The myth of self-esteem exists in part because American culture fosters an interest in an inner phenomenon we call the self. It also exists because sociologists and psychologists have made the self an object of their research and theory and have added the word to our vocabulary for discussion. I begin by examining the way in which contemporary people talk about the self and what they mean when they do so.

THE VOCABULARY OF SELFHOOD

To comprehend a myth we must understand something of the vocabulary people rely on to conceive of themselves and their world. Just as the biblical story of Job is expressed in a religious language in which "God" and "faith" and "obedience" are the key concepts, the myth of self-esteem is conveyed in a language that contemporary people understand and take for granted. No single word or concept is more important in this vocabulary than the word *self*. I will begin to examine the myth by attempting to uncover the meaning of this word.

The dictionary provides a useful starting point for this task, defining *self* in the following way:[1]

> self. 1. The total, essential, or particular being of a person; the individual . . . 2. The essential qualities distinguishing one person from another; individuality . . . 3. One's consciousness of one's own being or identity; the ego . . . 4. One's own interests, welfare, or advantage: thinking of self alone.

Dictionary definitions do not announce the undisputed meaning of words, but they do provide clues about how people use them. Practically speaking, a word's meaning lies in the way people use it in their everyday lives. The editor of this dictionary is telling us that people use the word *self* to designate the individual person and his or her total or essential being. Moreover, the nature of a person is thought in some way to lie in qualities that make him or her different from others; this essence is something of which people can be at least partly conscious; and consciousness of the self includes ideas about what is in the individual's interest as opposed to the interests of others.

To use the word *self* is to invoke this set of ideas. One may not necessarily intend to do so nor even be conscious of doing so. For example, a therapist—or perhaps a friend—might encourage you to "accept yourself for what you are." Someone who is anxious about the impression he or she will make on a prospective employer might be advised to "just be yourself." An individual might decline an invitation to a social occasion by saying "I need some time for myself." When we advise others to accept themselves, we are acting as though both they and we understand that the individual *has* something called a "self" that can be known and accepted, and that doing so often is a better course of action than attempting to change it. When we urge someone to "be yourself" or "be true to yourself" we express even more clearly a belief that each of us has an essential self, that it consists partly of qualities that make each of us unique, and that it is wise to cherish these qualities rather than imitate those of others.

The word *self* (along with the words we associate with it, such as "person" and "individual") thus provides a vehicle for our cultural understanding of human beings and their relationships to one another. The contemporary appeal of self-esteem depends upon these understandings, for it is because of the way contemporary vocabularies of the self encourage people to see themselves and their world that the conceptual entrepreneurs of self-esteem we will encounter in Chapter 3 have found success. Three main ideas seem particularly important to the American ethnopsychology of the self and the individual. First, it is widely believed that each person has a "true self," an inner essence that may be discovered or created, which defines the person's being. Second, people take for granted that the individual both needs and deserves recognition and acceptance from others. And third, Americans on the whole tend to think that the individual comes first—that the social world is the creation of individuals associating with one another and that it should be subservient to their needs.

The assumption of a true self amounts to a deeply held conviction that each person has an essential nature that shapes his or her conduct. Sometimes people refer explicitly to a "true self." More often, perhaps, they use other expressions that convey more or less the same idea: "the real me"; "who I really am"; "where I'm coming from"; "deep down inside"; "the kind of person I am." Whatever term or phrase is employed, the underlying idea is much the same: Something in each person marks or characterizes that person and shapes what he or she is capable of doing or is likely to do. There is some inner core, essence, kernel, nature, being, or substance that makes the person who and what he or she is.

The belief that each person possesses such a "true self" or a "real self" appears in a variety of ways in everyday life. "I am not myself today," a friend might say, excusing failure to do something promised. Although one might respond with a sarcastic question—"Who are you if you are not yourself?"—one is more likely to accept the excuse and not hold the friend's conduct against him or her. In doing so, one accepts the idea that something has interfered with the friend's capacity to act in a normal and socially desirable way. More important, one accepts the idea that such a capacity exists because the person has a true nature that, if allowed to express itself, would produce acceptable behavior.

The conviction that human beings have not only a deeply rooted need for recognition and acceptance but also a fundamental right to it takes many forms, but appears, perhaps most vividly, in the commonly heard plea to "Accept me for who I am." One hears this phrase, or something like it, in a great variety of social contexts and employed by diverse people. One hears it from adolescents in the throes of separation from their parents— from an anguished daughter, for example, caught between her (often mistaken) perceptions of what her parents want her to be and her urgent but as yet unformed sense of the person she wants to become. "I'm not like you, mother, and you'll just have to accept me for who I am." One hears the phrase spoken by the overweight, by alcoholics, by the poor, by the homeless, and by other socially stigmatized categories: I have accepted me for who I am; you should accept me for who I am.

Claims for recognition and acceptance range in tone from a demand to a plea, and sometimes, depending on the circumstances and social power of the user, mix the two. The adolescent tone of voice, for example, may be angry or defiant, but it is often tinged with pleading: *Please* accept me for what I am! Please understand I am an individual, not a clone of you, mother! "Accept me for what I am" makes a claim for a certain kind of social response or treatment, and even when couched in demanding tones there is an underlying plea for the validation of the self. When expressed in the most plaintive terms, there nevertheless is an implicit claim that the individual deserves a particular kind of social treatment and has the right to demand it.

Finally, the assumption that the individual comes first is such a pervasive part of our contemporary understanding of the world that it seems to be a self-evident truth rather than a culturally formed belief. In a liberal democracy, it is the individual who possesses rights—to life and liberty, for example, to the pursuit of happiness, to privacy, or to freedom of speech and religion. The state may make demands on the individual, but at least in principle the burden of proof falls upon the former. That is, the authorities must exercise "due process" in depriving an individual of his or her liberty as punishment for a crime. Individuals do not necessarily take for granted that they must sacrifice their own needs to those of their families or community, but often have to be persuaded to do so. Moreover, it is the individual who is blamed for failure and credited with success. Thus, we often tend to see poverty as the fault of the poor and wealth as the result of effort, in spite of evidence that people are disadvantaged or advantaged by circumstances such as race or gender or social class that lie well beyond their control.

In a society where the individual comes first, "looking out for number one" is not only an acceptable attitude to adopt but a matter-of-fact prediction of how others will behave. We tend to think it is natural for people to be "selfish" or "self-interested." As a result, we think of "teamwork" or "cooperation" not as natural or spontaneous forms of human conduct but as achievable only with effort and sometimes not at all. Athletes, we say, have to learn to "put the team first" or to "be team players." Cooperation requires "self-sacrifice," a willingness to forego individual achievement or reward. Even to speak of "teamwork" then is to bring to life our assumption that the individual comes first.

Putting the person ahead of society also reflects a belief that individuals have great powers and potential and that only the individual is capable of succeeding or achieving happiness. In this view, society cannot do for individuals what they will not do for themselves. It cannot make them accomplish great things if they do not wish to do so, and it cannot guarantee a satisfying life if they do not seek it themselves. The corollary is that individuals can achieve success and happiness if they want to. That is, *all* that it takes to achieve these things is the will to do so.

These assumptions about the self exert a powerful hold on our understanding of ourselves and the social world around us. Although they are, as we will see later, frequently challenged by contrasting ideas, they nevertheless dominate our thinking. And they remain deeply embedded in our language. As Robert Bellah and his associates pointed out in their book *Habits of the Heart*, individualism is the "first language" of Americans.[2] We find it easier to speak about "true selves" and "self-actualization" and "looking out for number one" than we do about the individual's debts or obligations to community or society, even when we recognize their importance.

The self is, in short, what social scientists nowadays often refer to as a social construction. That is, it is something brought into being by human beings as they act on the basis of their understandings and beliefs. Although it exists because of processes and capabilities that are common to human beings wherever they are found, what contemporary people call the "self" is a cultural and not a universal entity. The generalizations that both ordinary people and social scientists make about it are not mere factual statements about the nature of human beings and their world. The self constructed in contemporary American culture is, one might say, an invention rather than a discovery. Once invented—which is to say, once the assumptions I described earlier take hold—this socially constructed self seems as real and inevitable as anything in nature. The belief in a real self, the sense of entitlement to acceptance by self and others, and the assumption that the individual comes before the society seem to contemporary Americans to be obvious truths rather than cultural beliefs. And by acting on what we believe to be eternal truths about human nature, we tend to create the very evidence we need to verify them.

INDIVIDUAL AND SELF IN AMERICAN CULTURE

Contemporary American beliefs about the nature and power of the self are embedded in an American cultural tradition that has long celebrated the individual and regarded the community as the creation of individuals. The origin of American individualism is complex, and the very nature of this individualism has provoked a great deal of scholarly controversy. Even so, there is general agreement that individualism is central to an understanding of how Americans think about themselves and one another.

Several aspects of the American historical experience have favored the development of strong beliefs in the centrality and power of the individual person. The colonies that were to become the nucleus of the United States were founded by people on the move—whether Puritans seeking to establish a more perfect religious community or farmers and artisans eager to escape the limited opportunities of Europe. The country was peopled through successive waves of immigration—the voluntary migration of people seeking to find or build a better way of life, the forced migration of slaves from Africa, the economically or politically constrained migration of the jobless, the hungry, or the oppressed. The nation expanded relentlessly across the North American continent, pushing native peoples out of the way or simply killing them, and encouraging many to believe that when you could see the smoke from your neighbor's chimney, it was time to move on.

From the beginning, American culture fostered the idea that individuals could improve their own lives and make a better world. It created people who were willing to pull up stakes and move elsewhere, abandoning their home communities for the dream of something better someplace else. Indeed, sometimes people were required to build new communities and new cultures, whether they had been forcibly removed from their homes, as were slaves, or had come to America out of economic or political necessity. America was to be different, for not only individual men and women could get a fresh start in life but the country itself was a new start for humankind. The national ideology idealized a new kind of human being—a "New Adam"—who would overcome the problems of European society and create a new and more perfect social order.[3]

American culture fostered an intense emphasis on the individual, a focus that was to be echoed in a variety of American myths and stories: The diligence and hard work of the young Benjamin Franklin; pioneers on the Oregon Trail seeking the opportunities of the West; mythical heroes such as Paul Bunyan or John Henry; cowboy gunslingers who saved Western towns from the ravages of outlaws; the robust manliness of President Theodore Roosevelt; the supposed "rugged individualism" of industrialists such as Andrew Carnegie. Social characters such as these embody the virtues of the free, energetic, strong, brave, and determined individual who overcomes obstacles and achieves fame or wealth for the self and the family. The "self-made man," who claimed to have earned wealth and fame independently and felt obligated to no one, became a late nineteenth-century hero.[4]

The celebration of the individual and the conviction that individuals possess distinctive capacities are nowhere more powerfully expressed than in the essays of the nineteenth-century American philosopher and man of letters, Ralph Waldo Emerson. Particularly in his essay on "Self-Reliance," first published in 1841 and read by generations of Americans since then as an expression of our deepest beliefs, Emerson struck a chord that still reverberates in the American character.[5] His ideas influenced not only writers such as Henry David Thoreau and Walt Whitman, but also nourished thinkers such as William James, whose ideas about the self will be discussed later in this chapter.

Emerson's idea of self-reliance was focused mainly on the conviction that each individual possesses the capacity to experience the world afresh, think independently, come to his or her own conclusions about life, and create new things and new ideas. Each person has within himself or herself the intuitive capacity to perceive or grasp the truth, and one feels most satisfied and confident in what one perceives when one does so spontaneously. "Every man," Emerson wrote, "discriminates between the voluntary acts of his mind, and his involuntary perceptions, and knows that to his involuntary perceptions a perfect faith is due."[6] In other words, our unconscious impulses are more trustworthy than our conscious thoughts.

This is particularly so because, as Emerson argued, our individual intuitions are too easily overwhelmed by pressures to be and think like others.

> Society is everywhere in conspiracy against the manhood
> of every one of its members. . . . The virtue in most
> request is conformity. Self-reliance is its aversion. It loves
> not realities and creators, but names and customs.[7]

Individuals too readily surrender the authority of their own thoughts and ideas to the authority of society and its rules, customs, books, and doctrines. Accordingly, "Whoso would be a man must be a nonconformist."[8] Emerson's advice is straightforward: "Trust thyself: every heart vibrates to that iron string."[9] In more contemporary language that Emerson would nevertheless understand, society alienates its members from their great powers of perception and creativity. It convinces them that their own thoughts and deeds are of less worth than established doctrine and customs.

Emersonian "self-reliance" thus sets the individual somewhat apart from society, for the latter seeks to exact conformity in word and deed from its members. One should, therefore, distrust received opinion and be suspicious of established ideas, trusting oneself rather than the doctrines others believe. One should be prepared to believe that one's own ideas, opinions, and inclinations are the correct ones and that those fostered by society are erroneous. One should listen to one's inner voice and, again in more contemporary language, express one's "real self."

It is not difficult to see echoes of this Emersonian idea in the contemporary voices of self-esteem advocates we heard in the previous chapter. The young man who lifted himself from the degradation of drug abuse through self-esteem spoke of the need to like and respect yourself for who you really are rather than what others want you to be. Likewise, those who devise techniques to help nurses or managers "feel great about themselves" are to a considerable degree acting on the basis of an Emersonian idea of self-trust. Only if one feels good about oneself, in this view, can one liberate one's powers and do one's best work.

Emerson's ideas about the individual did not express the only point of view held by nineteenth-century Americans. Many of his ideas were developed during and immediately after the exuberant and optimistic Jacksonian Era, when the country was rapidly expanding westward and the land seemed filled with unlimited possibilities. Even then, unbridled individualism was not the only cultural voice Americans heard. Like people everywhere, those who had painstakingly built communities after coming to North America became attached to them and viewed the call to abandon their settled lives and move west with ambivalence.[10] Writers like Nathaniel Hawthorne, for example, viewed the dissolution of established communities and settled ways with alarm and wrote caustically of the emerging new culture of individualism and opportunism. The Civil War cast a shadow over the society, for among other things it made clear just how restricted American ideas of individual freedom and independence were.

Mainstream American culture celebrated the individual and made self-reliance a virtue. But there also were undercurrents of fear that people too readily abandoned tradition, that in "looking out for number one" they too easily overlooked the needs of others. Like the dominant themes of individualism, these counterthemes also are echoed in the contemporary discourse of self-esteem. Social scientists remind us that self-esteem depends upon the person's location in the social world and treatment by others and is not shaped entirely by what the person imagines it to be. Social critics argue that the emphasis on self-esteem places too much importance on the individual's right to self-esteem and not enough on what he or she does to earn the respect of others and of the self.

SOCIAL SCIENCE AND
THE LANGUAGE OF SELF

American culture thus rather naturally fosters the invention and use of terms pertaining to the self—both pro and con. An intense consciousness of and interest in the individual create a demand for words with which to explore and depict individual character and self-consciousness. A tendency to view individuals as unique and regard the individual and community as separate from one another strengthens that demand. And a lingering belief that an individual must in some way subordinate himself or herself to the needs of the community raises doubts in many minds about the individualism that seems to dominate American culture.

Where there is a demand for a good or service, economists tell us, producers will come forward to meet that demand. As we will see, people not only frequently think of and talk about themselves, but they do so in a language created by science, especially by psychology. Practitioners of that discipline have become what we might think of as the "wholesalers" of ideas about people. That is, they are the source of terms, theories, and images designed to make sense of human behavior and to improve the human condition. Although many times their ideas reach the public directly through their books and speeches, to a great extent the "retail" distribution of their ideas is in the hands of nonscientists who convert their ideas into popular language and promote them in various ways. I will refer to such people collectively as "conceptual entrepreneurs," since it is largely through their enterprise that the concepts of psychological and social science have entered our vocabulary. In Chapter 3 we will encounter several of them. First, however, we will explore how behavioral science has shaped our ways of thinking about ourselves.

From the founding of the United States through much of the nineteenth century, the vocabulary in which Americans conceived and discussed the individual was strongly influenced by religious ideas, created and promoted by religious authorities. The individual's place in the community was explained and justified in religious terms. And many of the concerns of individuals as individuals were focused on religious status, whether conceived as adherence to one's religious commandments in this world or in terms of one's fate in the next.

During the latter part of the nineteenth century, and extending into the twentieth century, science began to shape our conceptions of human beings and provide a new language for conceiving them. Although the origins of natural science extend well back into the seventeenth century, it was during the nineteenth century that the social and behavioral sciences emerged. The new vocabulary they created challenged religious conceptions of human beings, just as science itself had challenged older religious and philosophical ideas about the natural world. Religion had focused its attention on right conduct and the proper relationship of human beings to one another and God, but the emerging science of sociology sought to explain and find ways of coping with the wrenching changes brought about by industrialization. Religion had fostered intense concern with the "soul" and its "salvation," but the emerging science of psychology created new words (such as Freud's id, ego, and superego) and gave existing words (such as self and self-esteem) new meanings.

There was an additional source of demand for scientific ideas about the self.[11] During the early part of the twentieth century, industry and government increasingly turned to psychology for assistance in organizing and administering their activities. Intelligence tests, for example, were developed and received part of their impetus as a means of screening recruits to the military service during World War II. Later, industry turned to psychological testing and to a variety of psychological theories to recruit and retain "well-adjusted" workers. Just as the body became the province of medicine during the nineteenth century, the self became the province of psychology during the twentieth.

We can trace part of our contemporary understanding of self-esteem to the nineteenth century philosopher and psychologist William James. One of the founders of the school of philosophy known as pragmatism and the author of a highly influential textbook in psychology (first published in 1890), James described the self and self-esteem in strikingly modern terms. Because James's ideas influenced both social scientists and conceptual entrepreneurs from his era to our own and form the basis for many of our contemporary ideas about the self, we must examine them.

James begins his discussion of the self by pointing to a paradox:

> Whatever I may be thinking of, I am always at the same time more or less aware of myself, of my personal existence. At the same time it is I who am aware; so that the total self of me . . . [is] partly known and partly knower, partly object and partly subject . . .[12]

In other words, James is saying, the individual is both an active, conscious *subject* who is aware of the world and an *object* of that consciousness. James referred to these aspects of the self as the "Me" and the "I" and held that one had to understand the self as composed of both. It is the Me that will mainly concern us here.

The Me, the self of which we are aware, James maintained, has several constituent elements.[13] First, there is the "material me," composed of one's body, clothing, family, possessions, dwelling, and the like. When I think of myself, he argues, I think of those things and I find it hard to draw the line between what I call me and what I call mine. Second, there is the "social me," which consists of the recognition that one gets from other people. Human beings, James said, have

> . . . An innate propensity to get ourselves noticed, and noticed favorably, by our kind. No more fiendish punishment could be devised . . . than that one should be turned loose in society and remain absolutely unnoticed by all the members thereof.[14]

James thought the human desire to be "recognized" by others comes instinctively to us. That is, just as he thought our tendency to preserve life is instinctive, so too he thought our concern for the attention and approval of others is instinctive. We want to be recognized by people we admire or whose social standing is greater than ours, he maintains, but we are satisfied in a pinch with any recognition. Even gossip and scandal are better than nothing.

Because of the propensity to seek recognition, the individual has not one social self, James said, but rather as many social selves as there are individuals and groups about whose opinion he or she cares. We show a different side of ourselves to our friends than to our teachers, to our parents than to our employees. We allow ourselves to relax and use informal language among friends, but are alert to how we might seem to teachers and guard our language when we speak to them. We dutifully accept advice from parents and confidently give it to subordinates.

James conceived the self as made up of feelings and emotions as well as of material and social elements. He labeled these emotions as "self-complacency" and "self-dissatisfaction," but in essence he was writing about what we now think of as self-esteem. Human beings can feel proud, arrogant, filled with themselves, or conceited, but they can also feel modest, humble, shameful, or despairing. They can feel energized and ready to take on any challenge, but they also can lack any will or desire and feel intuitively convinced that they will succeed at nothing. These feelings about the self are as important and fundamental as emotions such as fear or anger.

Although each person tends to carry "a certain average tone of self-feeling" that seems independent of his or her experience, the normal basis of self-feeling is

> ... one's actual success or failure, and the good or bad
> actual position one holds in the world.[15]

How a person feels about himself or herself thus turns upon what we do and, crucially, how others receive or respond to what we do. Our self-esteem, in other words, comes significantly from the social world. The recognition we receive—or fail to receive—from others shapes how we feel about ourselves.

The social world is in this sense the source of self-esteem, but James also pointed out that it lies within the individual's power to control it. Self-esteem is influenced not only by the individual's success in accomplishing tasks or earning the approval of others but also by the "pretensions" or aspirations that underlie his or her efforts. To an athlete set on establishing a world record by running the fastest mile or clearing the highest hurdle, coming in second nearly amounts to failure. To the average flabby and overweight American, even completing a mile run would seem a major accomplishment and would bolster self-esteem. It follows that individuals can raise self-esteem either by meeting the expectations they set for themselves or by adjusting those expectations so that they are easier to meet. Likewise, because self-esteem depends on the approval of others, individuals can increase it either by doing what is required to secure approval or by seeking approval from those who are likely to give it.

James's ideas about the psychology of the self are not that far removed from our contemporary assumptions about the self. Although his view of the self as having a multiple reality does not give much support to a belief that each person has a "real self," he nonetheless emphasizes the importance of the self. Moreover, his ideas provide scientific legitimacy for the assumptions that human beings crave recognition and that the individual has considerable capacity to shape his or her own destiny by selecting the others from whom recognition will be sought and the basis on which he or she will seek it.

Two other intellectual figures of the late nineteenth and early twentieth centuries also shaped contemporary beliefs about the self. Sociologist Charles H. Cooley emphasized the emotional aspects of the self and developed the concept of the "looking glass self." Philosopher George H. Mead explained how the self originated in the social world. Their ideas strongly influenced the research of social psychologists, especially within sociology, and shaped our contemporary understanding of self-esteem.

Cooley's theory of the self is complex, but for our purposes two of its elements are particularly important. First, like James, Cooley viewed the self as an affective (or emotional) phenomenon and not merely a cognitive one. The experience of the self is of a feeling of "me" or "mine," an emotional attachment to what one is and to what belongs to one. This feeling energizes the individual's efforts and activities, so we experience ourselves not neutrally or as robots, but with emotion and feeling. Cooley likens the self to the nucleus of a cell, similar to the surrounding material out of which it is formed, but "more active and definitely organized." It is a key part of the mind.

Second, Cooley held that the self and its associated feelings are inherently social. "There is no sense of 'I,'" he wrote, "without its correlative sense of you, or he, or they."[16] The "looking glass self," which Cooley compared to the image we see when we look in a mirror, does not arise from our direct grasp of ourselves, but depends on our imagination of the other's judgment of us. In two of the most widely cited passages in his work, Cooley describes the origin and nature of our ideas about ourselves:

> A self idea . . . seems to have three principal elements: the imagination of our appearance to the other person; the imagination of his judgment of that appearance; and some sort of self-feeling, such as pride or mortification.

> The thing that moves us to pride or shame is an imputed sentiment . . . This is evident from the fact that the character and weight of that other, in whose mind we see ourselves, makes all the difference with our feeling. We are ashamed to seem evasive in the presence of a straightforward man, cowardly in the presence of a brave one, gross in the eyes of a refined one, and so on. We imagine, and in imagining share, the judgments of the other mind.[17]

In other words, Cooley says, we arouse feelings in ourselves by imagining the feelings the other holds toward us. We are thus tied to the social world, which supplies us with images of what others are and what we should be, as well as with the opportunities for social interaction in which the looking-glass self is formed.

George Herbert Mead, who was not a sociologist but a philosopher, provided a more complete account of the origins of the self.[18] Whereas Cooley emphasized the emotional component of the self and argued that even the young infant has the feeling of appropriation on which a rudimentary sense of self depends, Mead emphasized cognition and argued that the person has no self at birth. Rather, he said, the self develops over time as the child learns language and acquires the capacity to experience himself or herself from the vantage point of others. At first, the child develops the ability to play at the various social roles—such as the familial roles of mother, father, sister, and brother—and by doing so becomes, as Mead put it, an object to himself or herself. Children in this *play stage* of socialization enact the roles of first one person and then another, first doing something in one character and then responding as another character. Later, the child enters what Mead called the *game stage* of socialization, wherein he or she is able to display an organized grasp of the self in a particular situation by grasping his or her role in relation to that of the situation as a whole. The child in a game of tag, for example, is able to recognize himself or herself as "it" and to experience a self from the vantage point of the other children, who are seeking to avoid being tagged and becoming "it."

For Mead, then, the self is an object of thought and action, and its organization is supplied by the social world in which it participates. Individuals are able to grasp themselves not only from the standpoint of particular others or situations, but more generally from the standpoint of the community or society as a whole to which they belong. Each person has an organized sense of self because he or she is able to experience the self from the imagined perspective of the society as a whole. Mead referred to this perspective as the "generalized other," and through this term he meant to refer especially to the norms and values of the community to which the person belongs.

Cooley and Mead supplied much of the theoretical framework on which later generations of social scientists would build their research on self-esteem. Cooley retained William James's emphasis on the emotional component of the self, and his "looking-glass self" provided a striking and easily remembered phrase with which to characterize the nature of the self. Mead neglected the emotional side of the self, and did not emphasize self-esteem, but his work reinforced the idea that the self is a product of the social world and that the imagined appraisals of others shape the individual's experience of the self. Neither Mead nor Cooley were particularly sympathetic to an unbridled individualism. Mead gave decided priority to the community and its attitudes, and Cooley felt the individual must be both vigorous in his or her own sense of self and aware of and sensitive to the opinions of others.

Among those who built upon the founding ideas of Cooley and Mead was sociologist Morris Rosenberg, whose work on the self became widely known and imitated.[19] His work is important to us because it has been so widely cited by the conceptual entrepreneurs of self-esteem. Rosenberg formulated a readily understood definition of the nature of the individual's self-image, developed a widely used and imitated measure of self-esteem, and conducted extensive research into the impact of various social factors on the self. By doing so, he encouraged others to do related research and lent scientific legitimacy to the field.

Rosenberg argued that the self-image could be studied in the same way we study the attitudes people hold to a variety of objects. Just as we hold attitudes toward movies, political parties, or other people, he said, we hold attitudes toward ourselves. The self is a more important and salient object than other objects, of course, and Rosenberg argued that people are perhaps universally motivated to hold a positive attitude toward it. Moreover, he said, following the analyses of James, Cooley, and Mead, that the self-image is powerfully influenced by the social world—by the person's imagination of the appraisals of others.

One of Rosenberg's chief contributions to the study of self-esteem was to develop a straightforward, easily administered measure of self-esteem. He developed a paper-and-pencil measure that asked respondents to respond to ten statements by indicating whether they strongly agreed, agreed, disagreed, or strongly disagreed with each. These statements are worth quoting, for Rosenberg's self-esteem scale has been so widely used and imitated that more often than not when researchers and conceptual entrepreneurs talk about measured self-esteem they are talking about his measure or one like it.

Rosenberg developed and validated the following ten-item self-esteem measure:[20]

1. On the whole, I am satisfied with myself.
2. At times I think I am no good at all.
3. I feel that I have a number of good qualities.
4. I am able to do things as well as most other people.
5. I feel I do not have much to be proud of.
6. I certainly feel useless at times.
7. I feel that I am a person of worth, at least on an equal plane with others.
8. I wish I could have more respect for myself.

9. All in all, I am inclined to feel that I am a failure.

10. I take a positive attitude toward myself.

These statements cover a variety of attitudes the person might take toward himself or herself. They address the emotional aspects of the self (satisfaction, pride) as well as the cognitive, and they encompass the person's imagination of himself or herself in relation to others as well as more direct self-judgments. To arrive at a measure of self-esteem for statistical purposes, responses to the ten items were arranged into a "scale" that summarized each individual's level of self-esteem.

Rosenberg's work became famous not only because he successfully defined and measured self-esteem but also because he applied his methods to the study of adolescents and to the social experiences and backgrounds that favored the development of high or low self-esteem. Like others then and since, Rosenberg felt the period of adolescence posed particular difficulties for the individual's developing sense of self, and was, therefore, an important phase in the life cycle for studying self-esteem. By studying self-esteem as it developed in different contexts of social class, religion, neighborhood composition, and the like, he was able to not only validate the proposition that self-esteem is socially derived but also show which social experiences and contexts shape positive and negative self-images.

Another social scientist whose research has influenced our contemporary understanding of self-esteem is psychologist Stanley Coopersmith. Beginning a series of research in 1959, by 1967 he was ready to publish *The Antecedents of Self-Esteem*,[21] a book that set forth what many psychologists have since regarded as the definitive statement of the conditions that foster high self-esteem in children. Coopersmith studied the self-esteem of a large number of white, middle-class preadolescent children (aged ten to twelve) in Connecticut, using a variety of methods including a fifty-item self-esteem inventory, clinical evaluation using several psychological tests and a clinical interview, observation of subjects' behavior in the laboratory, and interviews and questionnaires given to subjects and their mothers.

Coopersmith discovered three chief antecedents of self-esteem:

> . . . total or near total *acceptance* of the children by their parents, clearly defined and enforced *limits,* and the *respect* and latitude for individual action that exist within the defined limits. In effect, we can conclude that the parents of children with high self-esteem are concerned and attentive toward their children, that they structure the worlds of their children along lines they believe to be proper and appropriate, and that they permit relatively great freedom within the structures they have established.[22]

Clear limits, Coopersmith found, provide children with a solid basis for evaluating their own activities and performances. Rather than being rigid or authoritarian, parents who set limits are more flexible and tolerant, get along better with one another, and provide models with which the child can more easily identify.

Coopersmith's research also debunked some commonsense assumptions about self-esteem. In spite of the importance of physical attractiveness and height in American society, he found no association between these attributes and self-esteem. Like Morris Rosenberg, he also found limited associations between self-esteem and wealth, education, and achievement. Such general standards, he observed, tell us little about how individuals will evaluate themselves. Rather, his research suggests the importance of the individual's immediate interpersonal environment—particularly parents—and the way they treat the individual. He repeatedly stressed that permissiveness, the creation of a tension- and demand-free environment—which many thought would promote self-esteem—actually would lower it. High self-esteem, he emphasizes, is associated with "greater demands, firmer regulation, and parental decisiveness."

ACTUALIZING THE SELF AND THINKING POSITIVELY

In addition to the scientific approach to the study of the self and self-esteem, grounded in Mead, Cooley, and James and carried on by Rosenberg, Coopersmith, and many others, two other significant developments in twentieth-century social thought have strongly influenced the contemporary vocabulary of the self. One was the "person-centered" psychology of Carl Rogers, and the related work of others such as Abraham Maslow, in the "humanistic psychology" movement. The other was the "power of positive thinking" touted most famously by Protestant minister Norman Vincent Peale, but reminiscent of a nineteenth-century idea known as "mind cure." The ideas espoused by both of these movements clearly echo in the beliefs many people hold about themselves and about the nature of human life, and they are conspicuous in some versions of the myth of self-esteem.

Humanistic psychology arose during the 1940s and 1950s in part as a response to and in disagreement with other approaches to psychology. Like sociology, psychology sought the objectivity (and the prestige) of the natural sciences, and one of the ways it did so was to rid itself of individual subjectivity as much as possible. Behaviorism, for example, which originated in the work of John Watson (who, while a graduate student at the

University of Chicago, was a friend of George Herbert Mead), sought to establish laws of human behavior. It looked for those laws in observable connections between environmental stimuli and the behavioral responses of the organism. Behaviorists avoided considering the subjective perceptions or experiences of the organism, arguing that they could not be studied objectively. Humanistic psychology rebelled against this approach by making the person's perception of experiences, including the experience of the self, central to their understanding of behavior and their efforts to influence it for the better.

Rogers, for example, argued that the person ordinarily tends to or wants to behave in ways that are consistent with the picture of the self that has emerged through the person's experience.[23] If a woman sees herself as calm and controlled, she will attempt to behave in accordance with this picture of herself. People are capable of inconsistent behavior, however, for their actions are shaped not only by the wish to live up to the self-concept but also by organic needs or desires of which they may well not be conscious. The woman with such a calm and controlled self-concept may erupt in anger occasionally as a result of her mistreatment by significant others. She feels an unconscious need to do so, but she is apt to "disown" this behavior, claiming it is "not herself." In such situations, psychological maladjustment exists; the person is in a state of psychological tension, and further threats to the self will only serve to make it more rigid and defensive.

On the basis of these and other premises, Rogers created what he called "client-centered" therapy. The object of the therapy is to provide the individual with a situation where the warm, supportive, accepting therapist makes it possible for the individual to explore unconscious feelings and discrepancies between these feelings and self-concept. By accepting everything the client says, the therapist encourages such self-exploration and gradually the client becomes able to assimilate previously threatening experiences into the self. In essence, since behavior is in one fashion or another linked to self-concept, the way to change behavior in therapy is to enable the person safely to change his or her self-concept.

The humanistic psychologists placed considerable emphasis on what they called the "self-actualizing" tendency in human beings.[24] The human being is an organism, and like any other organism has a set of needs that must be met. These needs include a need for self-esteem, which in Maslow's well-known "hierarchy of needs" comes to the fore after physiological needs (hunger and thirst) as well as needs for safety and "belongingness" have been met. The organism's needs are good, not evil. That is, in Maslow's view, healthy development means actualizing an essentially good human nature, striving to meet such basic needs. Pathology arises when these needs are in some way blocked. In other words, human beings are in some ways like plants which, given a source of nourishment and light, will naturally grow to fulfill—or actualize—their potential. It is the same with human beings, who under the right conditions will be able to fulfill their potential, to actualize themselves.

In Rogers' view of the individual seeking self-actualization, it is by and large the society that throws up obstacles and creates the conditions for pathology. Society impedes our natural growth, sets up requirements we cannot meet, and leads us to have self-concepts that are out of step with our needs. It leads us to deny our inner striving, to deny significant parts of our-selves, and therefore to actualize ourselves much less than we could. In his later publications, in fact, Rogers generalized his "client-centered ther-apy" into a "person-centered approach," in which people would treat one another by the same philosophy that his therapeutic method had encour-aged. By being open to one another, accepting one another, and making their world safe for one another, people would transform themselves into more thoroughly self-actualizing creatures and would thereby make a better social world. They would create a social world free of repressive insti-tutions, one in which such basic needs as self-esteem would be met, not thwarted.

Arising much earlier than humanistic psychology and differing from it in significant ways, "mind cure" shared an optimistic view of human nature and of the capacities of individuals.[25] "Mind cure" is a name for an assort-ment of popular psychologies and self-help ideas that arose in the latter part of the nineteenth century. Like contemporary self-help methods, in-cluding the myth of self-esteem, mind cure aimed to improve people's "health, wealth, and peace of mind."[26] It proposed methods whereby people could achieve well-being, overcome the anxiety of living in an emerging industrial society, and find happiness and success. All of these things lay within people's grasp, if only they could mentally organize themselves to achieve them.

Heavily tinged with Protestant theology (the mind's power to cure itself of ills and achieve wonderful results ultimately derived from God), this movement rested in part on the discovery of the unconscious in the late nineteenth century. Although we generally think of the unconscious forces that powerfully affect our lives as the discovery of Sigmund Freud, a num-ber of thinkers, including William James, had earlier wrestled with this con-cept. Mind cure emphasized the unconscious forces in human conduct, and indeed, regarded them as good. To achieve good things, the individual had to allow divine Truth to enter the unconscious mind. It was not through conscious intent or willpower that good would arrive, but through yielding the unconscious to the truth of God.

The last century has seen a large number of variations on the general theme of mind cure, and just as Americans today are a ready market for self-help books of all kinds, so they have been for at least a century and a half. One of the earliest versions of mind cure was Christian Science, founded by Mary Baker Eddy and still alive as a religious movement, perhaps most visible in the public eye because its members believe that sickness, being essentially a disease of the spirit, can be cured through faith. The theological component of mind cure gradually gave way to a more secular approach, and even where some theology was retained, it served largely secular purposes. Two examples out of scores of possibilities will illustrate the nature of this movement.

For a brief period, during the 1920s, the United States was taken by storm by French psychiatrist Emile Coué, who promoted a technique known as autosuggestion. Coué's approach, like that of the American proponents of mind cure, emphasized the role of the unconscious mind. "The unconscious self," he wrote, "is the grand director of all our functions." Moreover, he argued, "Every one of our thoughts, good or bad, becomes concrete, materializes, and becomes in short a reality."[27] Accordingly, one should put good thoughts into one's unconscious mind to create good realities.

At the height of the Coué fad, Americans everywhere were repeating his most famous positive thought: "Day by day in every way I am getting better and better." Coué's followers were to repeat this slogan twenty times a day, the object being to get it into the subconscious where it could direct good, successful actions. His books sold well, and in fact were reissued as recently as 1961.

An even more popular and enduring exponent of mind cure who adapted its theology to rather clearly secular purposes was Protestant minister Norman Vincent Peale, pastor of the Marble Collegiate Church in New York and author of a number of popular books. Perhaps the best-known of these is *The Power of Positive Thinking,* which when first published in 1952 quickly rose to the top of the best-seller list and stayed there for two years. Although Peale is now dead, his book continues to find a place on the religion and self-help shelves of bookstores.[28]

Peale's book has been called the "Bible of American autosuggestion." Like Coué's method of autosuggestion, Peale's advice emphasizes the power of the unconscious mind and stresses the power of words to shape it. Peale argued that faith in God was a requisite to success, for only that faith could unleash the power of the unconscious mind. Like Coué, Peale proposed a variety of exercises the individual could use to get positive thoughts into the mind and allow the unconscious to pursue them. These techniques involved the kind of methods typical of mind cure—identifying positive thoughts or ideas and incorporating them into easily remembered phrases that one could frequently recall and repeat to oneself.

Both self-actualization and mind cure place great emphasis on the individual, on individual happiness and success, and on the things individuals can or must do to achieve good ends. As critics then, as now, have alleged, such approaches to human betterment pay little attention to the society, except perhaps as a source of obstacles to happiness. They are not very much interested in achieving social change, except insofar as it might come about as a result of the improvement of individuals. Mark Twain, a caustic social critic in his time, chastised Christian Science for ignoring social needs for hospitals, schools, libraries, and such public institutions and for concentrating on the health of individuals. "I have hunted, hunted, and hunted," he wrote, ". . . and have not yet got upon the track of a farthing that the Trust has spent upon any worthy object."[29] Mind cure was then, as self help is now, concerned with the individual much more than with society.

FROM WHOLESALE TO RETAIL

The various strands of thought I have sketched are heavily responsible for our contemporary vocabulary of the self. It would not be accurate to say that the ideas of psychologists, sociologists, or mind-cure advocates have in any simple way "caused" this vocabulary. That would put too much influence in the hands of the people who created these ideas and too little in the society and culture in which they lived and worked and whose problems concerned them. It would be more accurate to say that people who have worked at various levels and at different times in creating these ideas have participated in creating this vocabulary. They have provided an idea here, elaborated on an existing cultural tendency somewhere else.

Thinkers like James, Cooley, and Mead, researchers like Rosenberg and Coopersmith, and clinicians like Rogers can be thought of as the wholesalers of the self. That is, they have created the basic ideas and findings on which contemporary exponents of the myth of self-esteem have relied. Promoters such as Coué and Peale move us closer to the retail channels of distribution, for they are less concerned with creating ideas and more focused on creating practices that may be sold to buyers of books and lecture audiences. They drew upon many of the ideas of nineteenth-century thinkers, but they had not yet adopted the language of self-esteem. In the next chapter we will directly encounter the retail market for the myth of self-esteem and meet some of its most prominent participants.

NOTES

1. *The American Heritage Electronic Dictionary.*
2. Robert N. Bellah, et al., *Habits of the Heart.* Berkeley, California: University of California Press, 1985.

3. See R. W. B. Lewis, *The American Adam: Innocence, Tragedy, and Tradition in the Nineteenth Century.* Chicago: University of Chicago Press, 1955.
4. See Irvin G. Wylie, *The Self-Made Man in America: The Myth of Rags to Riches.* New York: Free Press, 1954.
5. Quotations from "Self-Reliance" are taken from *The Essays of Ralph Waldo Emerson,* text established by A. R. Ferguson and J. F. Carr, introduction by Alfred Kazin. Cambridge: Belknap Press of Harvard University Press, 1987.
6. Ibid., 37.
7. Ibid., 29.
8. Ibid.
9. Ibid., 28.
10. I discuss some of these themes at greater length in *Dilemmas of the American Self* (Philadelphia: Temple University Press, 1989), especially in Chapter 3.
11. Niklas Rose, *Governing the Soul: The Shaping of the Private Self.* London: Routledge, 1990.
12. William James, *Psychology.* New York: World, 1948 [1892], 176. This book is James's abridgment of his *Principles of Psychology,* first published in 1890.
13. James also spoke of a "spiritual me," by which he did not mean a soul, but rather one's consciousness of oneself as a conscious being. The whole collection of one's thoughts and abilities can become an object of one's consciousness, and this constitutes the "spiritual me."
14. Ibid., 179.
15. Ibid., 182.
16. Charles Horton Cooley, *Human Nature and the Social Order.* New York: Scribner's, 1902, 141.
17. Ibid., 152.
18. George Herbert Mead, *Mind, Self, and Society.* Chicago: University of Chicago Press, 1934.
19. Morris Rosenberg, *Society and the Adolescent Self-Image.* Princeton: Princeton University Press, 1965.
20. Ibid., 305–307.
21. Stanley Coopersmith, *The Antecedents of Self-Esteem.* San Francisco: W. H. Freeman, 1967.
22. Ibid., 236.
23. Carl Rogers, *Client-Centered Therapy.* Boston: Houghton-Mifflin, 1951.
24. Abraham H. Maslow, *Motivation and Personality.* New York: Harper, 1954.
25. This discussion of "mind cure" draws upon Donald Meyer, *The*

Positive Thinkers, Rev. Ed. Middletown, Connecticut: Wesleyan
University Press, 1988.
26. Ibid., 13.
27. Emile Coué, *Self-Mastery through Conscious Auto-Suggestion.* New
York: Malkan Publishing Co., 1922, pp. 13, 25, 37. As quoted in
Donald W. Meyer, op. cit., 168.
28. Norman Vincent Peale, *The Power of Positive Thinking.* New York:
Prentice-Hall, 1952.
29. Mark Twain, *Christian Science.* New York: Harper and Brothers, 107,
75. As quoted in Meyer, op. cit., 102.

3

Conceptual Entrepreneurs

S ince the late nineteenth century, a virtual army of conceptual entrepreneurs have exploited the ideas we have just examined. The activities
of a few of them reveal the range of uses to which the concept of self-
esteem has been put and highlight its contemporary meanings. Because the
explosion of popular interest in self-esteem dates largely from the 1980s, I
will confine my attention to recent conceptual entrepreneurs.

The term *conceptual entrepreneur* derives loosely from Howard Becker's
analysis of moral enterprise.[1] Becker sought to explain why some forms of
behavior—such as the sale and use of marijuana and other drugs—become
the object of legislative prohibition and subsequent enforcement and punishment. During the 1930s, for example, marijuana became an illegal drug,
in spite of the fact that previously it had been largely ignored. Becker argued
that when forms of behavior previously tolerated become defined as
deviant, it usually is possible to find moral entrepreneurs at work. Moral
entrepreneurs are those who seek to have a particular activity defined as
deviant and who typically stand to gain if laws are passed against it. Laws
were passed making the sale and possession of marijuana illegal, Becker
argued, largely as a result of a campaign by officials of the Federal Bureau of
Narcotics. The Bureau, seeking to extend its influence and expand its budget, saw an opportunity to do so in the redefinition of marijuana as an illegal drug. If marijuana became illegal, some agency—namely, the Bureau—
would have to enforce the law and would get the necessary resources, thus
adding to the status and power of its officials.

Conceptual entrepreneurs are those who, in a similar way, seek to
develop and promote ideas about the solution of individual and social
problems. They typically focus on a single idea or concept—such as self-
esteem—and seek to persuade others that it has singular powers to make
individuals happier and the social world a better place. While moral entrepreneurs seek to promote ideas about right and wrong, conceptual entrepreneurs focus on solutions to problems. While social problems activists
seek to have specific social conditions, such as child-abuse or homelessness,

defined as problems, conceptual entrepreneurs offer ready-made solutions to conditions already defined as problems.

Conceptual entrepreneurship has four principal attributes. First, entrepreneurs engage in claims-making activities designed to persuade others about the importance of their discoveries. Second, they use scientific ideas, or what they claim to be the research findings of science, to argue the truth or legitimacy of their claims. Third, they promote specific programs or activities based on the central concept or idea, often adding their own particular proprietary twist to the underlying concept. And fourth, they stand to gain financially or in social status as a result of their activities.

Sociologists have come to understand that the definition of various social conditions as problems that need solutions always depends to a great extent on the activities of claims-makers.[2] These are individuals and groups—Mothers Against Drunk Driving, The Coalition Against Homelessness—who adopt a social problem as their concern and make various claims with respect to it. They claim the problem is important and pressing. They claim the right to speak on behalf of the victims of the problem and the duty to take action to improve their lives. They claim a share of the public's attention and public resources, arguing the importance of the problem and its priority over other problems. And they make claims about the nature of the problem, particularly about what causes it and what actions will be required to overcome it.

Conceptual entrepreneurs likewise make a variety of claims about their discovery of an important *solution* to human problems. Self-esteem entrepreneurs, particularly those who argue that low self-esteem lies at the root of such problems as drug use, educational failure, or teenage pregnancy, tend to claim the status of victim for those whose lives they seek to improve. And with the claim that, for example, many children are victimized by a society whose values and practices lower their self-esteem, comes the implicit claim that those who speak on behalf of self-esteem have the right and duty to speak on behalf of these victims. Claims about self-esteem also tend to make it central to the solution of problems. Educators who believe in the importance of self-esteem, for example, often argue that the self-esteem of children must be improved before other educational problems can be solved. And because conceptual claims-making focuses on solutions rather than problems, the claims of self-esteem entrepreneurs tend to focus on the specific methods that must be employed to improve self-esteem.

Claims-making requires some means through which entrepreneurs can reach their intended audiences. Self-esteem entrepreneurs have employed a variety of communication media and organizational strategies. They write books about self-esteem and the techniques for improving it. They publish articles in magazines and professional journals whose audiences include parents, teachers, nurses, farmers, bankers, writers, corporate managers, and just about any other group one can imagine. They market an array of videotapes and audiotapes, "seminars," and therapy sessions, using televised "infomercials," advertisements in alternative newspapers, listings in guides to holistic healing, and, more recently, in "home pages" on the World Wide Web. They use existing platforms and organizations and create new ones. In the 1980s, for example, a member of the California legislature, John Vasconcellos, successfully argued for the establishment of a state Task Force on Self-Esteem and Social and Personal Responsibility, about which we will hear in detail later.

We can gain some appreciation of the explosion of interest in self-esteem and of the accompanying activities of conceptual entrepreneurs by looking at the sheer number of articles and books that focus on the topic. The Educational Resources Information Center (ERIC) computerized index of articles in education shows a dramatic increase in articles dealing with self-esteem since 1966 (when the index began). From 1966 through 1981, a search for articles with self-esteem in the topic or title yields an average of about 150 articles per year. For the decade 1982 through 1991, the yearly average more than doubled to about 323 articles. And for the period 1992 to the first half of 1996, the yearly average increased to 492 articles. The index lists a total of 7,836 articles for the period 1966 through the first half of 1996. A similar computerized search in the Psychinfo index reveals a similar pattern: From 1967 through 1983, the index shows an average yearly production of 272 articles dealing with self-esteem; for the years 1984 through 1993, the yearly average is 668 articles. And the widely used INFOTRAK database, which includes articles in both popular and academic sources, likewise shows an increase in article production. From the beginning of its indexing in 1982 through 1986, INFOTRAK indexed only thirteen articles dealing with self-esteem. Thereafter, the yearly totals increase, averaging eighty-three articles yearly by the early 1990s. A check of the card catalogue at the University of Massachusetts, Amherst, shows a similar pattern for books: during the 1980s, the catalogue lists about six new entries each year dealing with self-esteem; during the first half of the 1990s, the figure more than doubles to a yearly average of nearly thirteen.[3]

Claims-makers must establish their legitimacy. Especially since the 1980s, the conceptual entrepreneurs of self-esteem have sought legitimacy in the theories and research findings of social science, particularly psychology. The thousands of articles produced by social scientists since the 1960s have not only fueled the interest of conceptual entrepreneurs and provided them with material, but also have provided a source of authority for their assertions.

This vast body of research studies and theories no doubt posed a problem for claims-makers, for its findings were couched in the careful and sometimes complex language of science. Social scientists, obeying the

norms of scientific work, have for the most part been careful not to generalize beyond the data they have gathered. Where evidence was inconclusive
or contradictory, they said so. Claims-makers, however, quite naturally
regarded the careful language of science as being rhetorically weak. To
establish the validity and importance of their ideas in the public realm, they
needed simple facts, not complex scientific findings. They extracted and
emphasized such facts as they could, ignoring the qualifications. Wanting to
show how social class or race could injure self-esteem, for example, they
extracted this "fact" from the research literature, conveniently ignoring
the important qualification that whether class or race affects self-esteem
depends on the social context in which children are raised and the significant others with whom they compare themselves. Claims-makers also recognized that science confers legitimacy not just by establishing facts but
also through the authority of the individual scientist. As a result, the conceptual entrepreneurs of self-esteem gradually canonized the work of a few
social scientists, most notably Morris Rosenberg in sociology and Stanley
Coopersmith in psychology. Books and articles about self-esteem would
attribute a set of "facts" to these authors and praise their scientific accomplishments. The stature of the social scientist would then substitute for evidence that would substantiate the "facts."

Conceptual entrepreneurs also misused scientific research in another
critical way. Many of the findings about self-esteem on which they rely consist of correlations between paper-and-pencil measures of self-esteem
(such as those developed by Rosenberg) and various individual and social
characteristics. Individuals' self-esteem scores can be correlated with age,
gender, social background, school performance, delinquency involvement,
and other matters of interest to the researcher. Social scientists understand
that statistical correlations do not establish causality. If, for example, students who do better in school tend to have higher self-esteem scores, we
cannot assume that their higher self-esteem causes their better performance. It might just as likely be the case that they have higher self-esteem
because they do better in school. Self-esteem entrepreneurs have been
prone to overlook this crucial fact and wrongly treat correlational evidence
as proof of causality.

Once a general idea has been "discovered" by conceptual entrepreneurs
and given scientific legitimacy, the way is open for the invention of means
to put their discovery to use. If self-esteem lies at the root of many problems
and is an efficacious solution, then entrepreneurs are free to create and
market programs that will, they claim, enhance self-esteem. They have been
highly inventive in doing so. As we will see in this chapter and the next, a
variety of entrepreneurs have been prolific inventors of methods that supposedly enhance self-esteem.

This process of invention and discovery takes place in a social and cultural context that has been particularly favorable for purveyors of self-esteem remedies. There are few restrictions, for example, on who can market self-esteem or what specific remedies they can recommend. Although one must be licensed to call oneself a psychologist, there are few legal restrictions on those who invent various forms of therapy and charge clients who wish to benefit from it (or other potential therapists who wish to learn how to administer it). Moreover, self-esteem has been marketed in a culture that has been very receptive to self-help books of any kind. A visit to a large bookstore in my vicinity, for example, revealed about 100 feet of shelf space devoted to various psychologically oriented self-help books. Do-it-yourselfers who want to remodel a kitchen or add a deck have to make do with a selection of books that occupies perhaps one-tenth the space.

Finally, conceptual entrepreneurship carries the possibility of wealth, fame, appearances on television talk shows, and other forms of material and status gain. In a culture that is so receptive to therapy, self-help books, and other forms of advice, self-esteem is not only marketable but so is the self-esteem expert. It is, in other words, a potential avenue to wealth and fame, and perhaps, more elusively, a potential avenue to a status as a cultural "guru," one to whom the psychologically suffering and afflicted turn to for help and guidance.

A CORNUCOPIA OF SELF-ESTEEM

The tidal wave of popular articles and books that formed in the middle of the 1980s and continued through the mid-1990s produced an astonishing and often amusing variety of ways for individuals to enhance their own, their friends', or their children's self-esteem. Magazines whose audiences consisted of advice-seeking parents, professionals, managers, women, and almost every other social category to which specialized publications are addressed, found a ready supply of articles. Clinical psychologists and others offering individual therapy published books and audio cassette tapes promoting their methods. And as the Internet became a household word in the 1990s, self-esteem established itself in thousands of "home pages" on the World Wide Web.

Not surprisingly, a great many of the books and magazine articles on self-esteem are directed toward parents concerned with their children's well-being. Since 1980, for example, *Parents' Magazine* has published many articles advising parents about the various techniques for enhancing self-esteem and the pitfalls to be avoided in raising children to develop a healthy self-esteem. Sometimes these articles offer specific techniques parents may use to develop self-esteem in their children. One, for example, advises that "Children need to be commended for what they do and who they are, and praise that addresses their individual needs, style, and performance is the most valuable kind."[4] Another suggests that either the parent or teacher develop a "balance sheet" of things the child does well and things he or she does not, and use it to convince the child to think better of himself or herself.[5]

Other articles directed toward parents seem more focused on the nature and good consequences of self-esteem and provide only general guidance about how to enhance it. One author, who like many others uses "self-esteem" virtually as a synonym for the child's sense of competence and self-confidence, asserts that there are four conditions that produce self-esteem. The child will develop competence if he or she "has a close, warm relationship with an adult," and has "interesting surroundings," "ample opportunity to interact with other people," and has a "responsive" environment.[6] And as another author describes it, self-esteem is the font of many virtues.

> It provides the basis for intimacy, for creativity, for satis-
> faction, effective functioning, and involvement in con-
> cerns that go beyond self interest, and for acceptance of
> others.[7]

Although couched in general terms rather than in how-to-do-it specifics, such articles nonetheless are engaged in marketing self-esteem. They are, in effect, the equivalent of institutional advertising—selling the image of the corporation rather than a specific product. Just as the Rockwell Corporation's advertising campaign asserts that "We don't make the products you buy, we just make them better," general articles about self-esteem sell the idea of self-esteem, not a particular method for improving it.

Articles declaiming either the importance of self-esteem or a specific method for enhancing it also frequently attempt to reassure parents about their own competence. Parents who rely upon the advice of experts in raising their children find a measure of security in doing what the experts recommend, but such advice is also a potential source of anxiety. Parents may worry about whether they are using the latest and best advice, or are implementing it properly. After discussing various techniques for encouraging self-esteem, one author reassures readers that "encouraging self-esteem is not nearly as precise and difficult as I have made it sound."[8] Whatever their shortcomings in technique, parents who intend or desire to support their children's self-esteem will generally do the right thing.

It is not only children who can benefit from their parents' learning appropriate techniques, for self-esteem is considered useful across a wide spectrum of organizations and occupations. One author recommends the importance of a good self-image for farmers, who have, in the author's opinion, "planted the wrong kind of self-image seeds" and allowed self-esteem to be dictated by the weather. There is one skill, says this "professional keynoter, seminar leader, and human resource consultant," that will crucially affect success, and it is not the farmer's information about "weeds, seeds, feeds, and breeds" on the farm. Rather, the skill consists of knowing how to "develop and maintain a positive self-image." And much of this skill involves replacing negative and self-defeating thoughts with positive ones, by listing and forgetting past mistakes, listing and repeating personal strengths and assets, reading or listening to "something motivational or inspirational every day," listing specific goals, and taking responsibility for one's emotional environment. The farmer who does so will be in charge of his or her own self-esteem, and will sow seeds of self-concept that will yield agricultural fruits.[9]

Bankers, too, can profit by cultivating self-esteem in potential customers, for example, in a situation where a customer in difficult economic circumstances needs credit. The banker wants to extend a loan or stretch out the repayment of an existing loan so his or her customer's business can succeed. But at the same time the banker needs to protect the bank's interest and either collect the loan or at least cut its losses. A professor of psychology advises that it is important not to do anything to lower the customer's self-esteem, because the banker has a certain responsibility in "maintaining the individual's self-worth in the face of declining net worth." A customer whose self-esteem is high is more likely to repay the loan and to be a satisfied customer, for he or she will be competent, ambitious, competitive, and motivated to succeed. Therefore, the banker must accentuate the positive, eliminate the negative from comments to the customer, provide positive appraisals of the customer, and show respect.[10]

High self-esteem doesn't just fill the coffers of the bank. One management consultant argues,

> Even the amount of money a person earns is controlled by
> his or her self-concept.[11]

To earn more money, you must believe you will earn more; and if you do, the rest of the world will come around to your point of view! This advice takes to the secular heart the most wildly optimistic version of "positive thinking" supplied by Norman Vincent Peale, but lacks Peale's emphasis on God as the source of good things and the entity in whom one must have faith in order to think positively. In the management version, all good things come to the person who merely thinks positively of self.

Although management advice about self-esteem often has a utilitarian cast, there also are powerful expressive elements. In his advice to high-tech corporations, for example, one author defines the "barometers of self-esteem." Among other things, self-esteem rests on the following:

> Clear evidence we are valued and cared about through
> warm empathic relationships; open two-way communi-
> cation expressing not only facts but also feelings. . . . Per-
> sonally acting congruent with our deeply held values and
> beliefs; association with individuals and organizations
> who similarly behave in accordance with our values.[12]

Self-esteem is enlisted in the interests of the manager and the corporation, but the expressive subjectivity of the employee is considered important. He or she must be able to "communicate," express "feelings" as well as facts, and act on the basis of personal beliefs and not merely on the basis of corporate needs or dictates. Here we see not merely positive thinking, but echoes of humanistic psychology's emphasis on self-actualization.

Some proposals for enhancing self-esteem have a playful quality. One writer—I imagine her as a Martha Stewart for the psyche—creates magical gift jars of self-esteem. These consist of old Swiss Miss chocolate powder cans (complete with chocolate aroma) filled with slips of paper on which bracing messages are written about the recipient's virtues. It might seem insincere merely to tell another of one's liking, she opines, but friends find it hard to ignore her magical jars. She recommends writing compliments that are concrete and that relate to the person's interests or talents. For a tennis player, for example, she would write "Chris Evert Lloyd has nothing on you." She recommends the use of humor: "You are so fair and beautiful that Snow White is making poisoned apples with your name on them." Comments, the author maintains, should refer to the relationship between the sender and recipient: "Had you never come into my life, to be my friend, my life would be far poorer for your absence." The author provides her "Emergency Supply of Self-Esteem" as a combined greeting card and gift designed to enhance the self-esteem of friends. But knowing that the effort will help "heal someone's inner hurts" or even "change her life for the better" can also "do a lot for your self-esteem."[13]

Some conceptual entrepreneurs offer not merely an article placed here or there in advice magazines but rather an entire product line. One such entre-preneur is Shad Helmstetter, Ph.D., creator of "The Self-Talk™ Solution" and author of at least six books of advice to parents and others.[14] In addition to his books, Helmstetter offers a selection of audiocassettes for children and teenagers (at $49.50 per set), markets a self-help seminar, and maintains a World Wide Web site to provide information and sell his products.

We are programmed by our social experiences, Dr. Helmstatter argues, to hold erroneous and self-defeating beliefs about ourselves. Because we act on the basis of these beliefs, we accomplish less than we could, and we feel driven to do unproductive and damaging things, such as using drugs or eat-ing more than we want to eat. The solution to our problems—and the route to self-esteem—thus lies in changing our beliefs about ourselves. Self-Talk™ is advanced as a method for doing so. By listening to positive statements about oneself, one learns to recognize the negative and self-defeating beliefs one holds. As one listens to positive statements, one begins to internalize such ways of talking about oneself, and the result is an improved outlook on life. By hearing, thinking, and repeating positive statements, one reprograms one's beliefs.

Although Norman Vincent Peale's message of positive thinking is heard much less often these days, one well-known contemporary religious figure influenced by Peale easily qualifies as a self-esteem entrepreneur. He is Robert Schuller, television minister of the "Hour of Power" and pastor of the "Crystal Cathedral" in Garden Grove, California, who makes self-esteem a central feature of his religious message. Amidst the splendor of his stupendous glass church, part of which swings open to accommodate those looking for drive-in religion and self-esteem, Schuller preaches a message of "God's Power Within You" and the goal of thinking positively. A handsome man, perpetually beaming at his affluent congregation who presumably already benefit from thinking positive thoughts, he also preaches a doctrine of self-esteem. Self-esteem, he says, is not praise of oneself for what one is but rather "the divine dignity that God intended to be our emotional birthright as children created in his image." It is his method, he says, to "treat all people as beautiful human beings even if you know—and especially if you know—how bad they are." Such treatment—such fostering of self-esteem—is part of his method of inducing people to seek salvation. Better, he argues, to bolster their self-esteem and get them in the door of the church, than to repel them with immediate news of their sinfulness. Self-esteem—which they will learn was "lost in the Garden"—can only be regained through faith in Christ.[15]

Writing on a World Wide Web page maintained by the Campus Crusade for Christ, Darla Walker echoes Schuller's message and manages to integrate it with contemporary thinking about self-esteem. Directing her views toward women—the Web page is titled "Women and Self-Esteem"—Walker asserts some of the standard ideas of the self-esteem movement. A temporary sense of self-esteem can be had, she writes, when people find themselves in loving relationships, are never criticized, succeed financially, or receive recognition from their peer groups. But it is false to assume that these conditions really guarantee self-esteem, for they provide only a fleeting sense of worth, not the stable and enduring sense of being loved and accepted.

Real self-esteem is only to be had through faith in God, who, she says, created the need for self-esteem and also created the means for achieving it. "God is the only One," she writes, "who knows me totally, and loves me totally. I never have to fear He'll learn something about me that's so bad that

he'll reject me." Women cannot achieve real self-esteem through their relationships or accomplishments, but only through a right relationship with
God. Taking her cue from generations of positive thinkers who assert that
"the way we think largely determines the way we behave," she argues that
women must retrain themselves to learn what is true about them and will
always be true. That is, each is a significant person to God, and each is loved
unconditionally, regardless of what is accomplished.[16]

This varied assortment of goodies in the self-esteem cornucopia is only
a sample of what is available on the market. To get a firmer fix on the activities and ideas of the conceptual entrepreneurs of self-esteem, we must look
at some of them in greater detail. Sunny California, the land of self-esteem,
as well as milk and honey, is a good place to begin.

CALIFORNIA ESTEEMIN'

In 1986, the state legislature of California created the "California Task Force
to Promote Self-Esteem and Personal and Social Responsibility." The project was promoted by Assemblyman John Vasconcellos, who had discovered
the concept of self-esteem a few years earlier and became convinced that it
was the key to the solution of a host of social problems, ranging from
teenage pregnancy to drug addiction to child abuse. Armed with $735,000
in state funds, the Task Force quickly became a topic of public discussion, a
good deal of it satirical or sarcastic. Social critics regarded it as another
instance of a cultural madness to be expected in California—"touchy, feely,
dopey," as one commentator put it. Cartoonist Gary Trudeau lampooned
the effort in the Doonesbury comic strip, appointing Barbara ("Boopsie")
Boopstein to his imaginary version of the Task Force. In spite of widespread
derision, the Task Force also found 400 Californians eager to become members, and it set about its assigned tasks of identifying the role of self-esteem
in creating social problems, compiling existing knowledge on how self-
esteem is developed, damaged, and restored, and identifying model programs for the enhancement of self-esteem.

The conceptual entrepreneur behind the formation of the Task Force,
John Vasconcellos, was (in his words) a "high-achiever" who became a
"prominent lawyer in a prestigious firm." In 1966, he ran successfully for
the state legislature and was repeatedly reelected to office. In spite of his
successes, he confesses, he had ". . . almost no sense of myself, no self-
esteem."[17] He sought success in order to please other people, but constantly
felt "guilt-ridden and ashamed, constantly beating my breast and professing
my unworthiness." "Awakening painfully to this problem" in 1966, he began
a quest to gain back his self-esteem, undergoing various forms of therapy,
and he began to focus not only on his own self-esteem but also began a

quest to enable others to develop theirs. When he became chair of the State Assembly's Ways and Means Committee in 1980, responsible for reviewing the state's annual budget, he realized how much money and effort was spent on "containment and remediation" of social problems and how little was spent on their prevention. In 1984, he introduced legislation that would involve the state government in an effort to determine whether self-esteem might be the "social vaccine" that would prevent such problems and save the state money in the long run. After some initial setbacks, including a veto by the governor, the legislation creating the twenty-five member Task Force was passed and signed into law in the fall of 1986.

The beliefs that underlie Vasconcellos's convictions about the importance of self-esteem appear to owe most to the ideas of Carl Rogers. Vasconcellos reports hearing Rogers assert at a dinner party that ". . . we human beings are innately inclined toward becoming constructive and life-affirming and responsible and trustworthy."[18] It is such a view of human nature, he says, that underlies the work of the self-esteem movement. For Vasconcellos, self-esteem involves ". . . a deeply felt appreciation of oneself and one's natural being, a trust of one's instincts and abilities."[19] People who have self-esteem, he argues, are able to live ". . . generously and peacefully, without delinquency or destructiveness, encouraging one another in our lives and our growth."[20] In other words, self-esteem appears to be a good indicator of the self-actualizing tendency. People who appreciate themselves are able to grow, like flowers, toward the natural light of goodness and "personal and social responsibility."

The Task Force was given three charges by the legislation that created it. First, it was to examine research evidence on the possible role of self-esteem in the areas of crime and violence, drug abuse, teenage pregnancy, child abuse, welfare dependency, and educational failure. Second, it was to gather knowledge about the factors that encourage or damage self-esteem. And third, it was to create an inventory of successful programs and institutions to which people could turn in an effort to improve self-esteem.

One of the products of the Task Force's work, in response to its first charge, was a book reporting on the empirical evidence for and against the importance of self-esteem as a causal agent in the several problem areas with which the Task Force was concerned. The book was edited by Andrew M. Mecca, the Task Force's chair, John Vasconcellos, and Neil J. Smelser, a distinguished sociologist at the University of California, Berkeley. Its chapters, which compile and assess research on the relevance of self-esteem in each of the problem areas, were written by a number of academic researchers, practitioners, and activists.

Considering their high expectations and strong beliefs in the importance of self-esteem, it is hard to believe the Task Force members were not disappointed by the research findings. In every problem area, there was some evidence linking self-esteem to the problem. But, as Smelser puts it, the most consistent report in the chapters is that ". . . the associations between self-esteem and its expected consequences are mixed, insignificant, or absent."[21] Smelser makes a valiant effort to rescue the concept of self-esteem, expressing his own intuitive belief that it is an important variable in explaining and solving various social problems. He points out the difficulties of measuring self-esteem, as well as the numerous other factors that may operate along with self-esteem in creating social problems.

Having pointed to the disappointing findings about the correlation between self-esteem and social problems, and having attempted to explain why the relationships are weak or nonexistent, he also makes clear that there is even less evidence for a causal relationship between self-esteem and the various problems. Correlation, whether weak or strong, does not establish causality, he points out. Even if there were a correlation between the self-esteem of adults and their tendency to abuse children (and there is not), for example, such a correlation would not establish that low self-esteem is the cause of child abuse. Both the low self-esteem and the abuse might be the consequence of other factors.

It is fascinating to discover that the rather poor showing of self-esteem as an explanatory and causal variable in the array of social problems on which the Task Force focused did not seem to dampen the members' enthusiasm for the importance of self-esteem. Smelser's scientific commitments lead him to specify how better research might be conducted in the future and to urge caution with respect to the formulation of public policy based upon ideas about self-esteem. But the Task Force continued its work, and press reports on the results of its efforts did not on the whole seem to emphasize the inconclusive nature of its findings. *Time* magazine called the recommendations of the Task Force's final report ("Toward a State of Esteem") to offer parenting courses to teenagers and to require courses in self-esteem of prospective teachers "sensible."[22] Even the *Christian Science Monitor,* which expressed concern that an emphasis on self-esteem could "pull toward self-centered thinking," urged readers to "take seriously the earnestness of the report." "Society does benefit," it argued, "from people who see and express more fully their deeper capacities, and who work to bring this out in others."[23] It is worth noting that seven members of the Task Force dissented from the final report for various philosophical, religious, and practical reasons, including its promotion of self-esteem as a universal remedy.

One result of the California Task Force was the creation of a social movement organization dedicated to "integrating self-esteem into the fabric of American Society." First named the National Council for Self-Esteem, the organization later changed its name to what it regarded as the more inclusive National Association for Self-Esteem (NASE). Like other such membership organizations, the National Association sought to develop a national body of dues-paying members who would receive its newsletter, participate in local self-esteem "chapters," and spread the gospel of self-esteem in their communities. Billing itself as "the largest and fastest growing self-esteem organization in the United States," NASE has sponsored national conferences that bring together self-esteem experts and organization members and promoted such activities as "Self-Esteem Week" and "Random Acts of Kindness Week."

NASE is a politically and philosophically diverse movement organization, a fact best revealed by the range of members of its advisory board. Feminist author Gloria Steinem, whose work I will shortly examine, is a member. Converted to the self-esteem movement somewhat to her surprise, as a feminist committed to social change and not simply personal transformation, she shares membership on this board with others whose philosophies are strikingly different. Jack Canfield, for example, markets ideas about self-esteem in education (which we will consider in the next chapter) that in some ways exemplify the "touchy, feely, dopey" aspect of the self-esteem movement. And Nathaniel Branden, formerly the associate of author Ayn Rand and a supporter of her philosophy of "objectivism," also is a member of the board and the author of books on self-esteem. Branden, however, makes it clear that although self-esteem is a crucial human need, it is not about "feeling good" but about real accomplishment. In a letter "To My Colleagues in the Self-Esteem Movement," Branden recommends a series of books by such conservative authors as Thomas Sowell and Charles Murray.[24] The NASE umbrella evidently shelters people whom one might expect to be at least mildly uncomfortable in one another's company!

FEMINISM DISCOVERS SELF-ESTEEM

In 1991, the American Association of University Women (AAUW) funded a widely publicized comparative study of gender discrimination in education. The study, "Shortchanging Girls, Shortchanging America," identified a variety of ways in which the educational system favors boys. Boys receive more of the classroom teacher's time and attention, the survey found, and more is expected of them. When boys fall short of expectations, teachers blame lack of effort, whereas they attribute girls' failure to lack of ability. As a result of these and other conditions, the self-esteem of girls falls precipitously during the junior high school years. Entering adolescence as spirited and self-confident girls, the subjects of the study often emerged as defeated young women lacking a belief in themselves and their abilities.

The AAUW study was widely publicized in the mass media. News reports focused particularly on the decline of self-esteem, which was headlined in newspapers and television news broadcasts. It was the first indication that feminists, concerned with the unequal treatment of women, had discovered self-esteem. Not long afterward, the well-known feminist author and founder of *Ms.* magazine, Gloria Steinem, wrote the best-selling *Revolution From Within: A Book of Self-Esteem,* detailing her personal discovery of the importance of self-esteem. Later still, in 1994, Peggy Orenstein wrote *Schoolgirls,* a book stimulated by the AAUW and written in cooperation with that organization. The book was based on a large number of interviews and observations in two California schools during the 1992–93 school year.

The discovery and promotion of self-esteem by these feminists came as an uncomfortable surprise to many of their followers, as it did to Steinem and Orenstein. Like the majority of feminists, they were convinced that improving the position of women in American society would require structural changes. It was not enough that women be motivated to succeed or that they aspire to careers they had previously shunned. Barriers would have to be removed and opportunities created, so women could actually act on their motivations and realize their aspirations. Hence, feminists were skeptical of explanations of inequality that placed or seemed to place any of the blame on the shoulders of women themselves. The emphasis on self-esteem, which had become culturally widespread by the beginning of the 1990s, seemed to them to be at least in part an explanation that "blamed the victim."

Near the beginning of her book, Gloria Steinem describes an incident that occurred to her at the Plaza Hotel in New York City in the late 1960s. Waiting in the lobby for the arrival of a visiting celebrity whom she was to interview, she was firmly escorted out the door by the hotel's assistant manager, who told her loudly that "unescorted ladies" were not allowed in the lobby. (As absurd as it seems, it was the practice in many hotels to exclude "unescorted ladies" from lobbies on the grounds that they might be prostitutes.) Steinem waited outside the revolving door, but her celebrity never arrived. One month later, she found herself in the same hotel lobby, on her way to interview another celebrity. This time, however, she lingered in the lobby, and when approached by the same assistant manager, she confronted him, asserting her right to be there, unescorted or not. Between these two occurrences, she reports, "Only one thing was different: my self-esteem." It had been raised, she goes on to relate, by experiences with her feminist colleagues during the intervening weeks. The second experience in the lobby, she reports, was her ". . . first inkling that there is a healthier self within each of us, just waiting for encouragement."[25]

Praising the existence and work of the California Task Force (and seeming not to recognize the precariousness of its findings about self-esteem), Steinem argues that self-esteem is a universal human experience and need. Every language has some word for it, she says, and some conception of "self-wisdom and self-honor as a source of strength, rebellion, and a kind of meta-democracy—a oneness with all living things and with the universe itself." We must return to such a conception of oneness, she says, ". . . that preceded patriarchy, racism, class systems, and other hierarchies that ration self-esteem." To do so would constitute a "revolution from within," for it would assert the individual's "natural and internal wisdom" against the demands of external authority.[26] It is the "true self" and the "inner voice" that is damaged or stilled by patriarchy, Steinem asserts, and while the restoration of self-esteem by itself is not enough to overcome it, little can happen without that restoration.

Like Steinem, Peggy Orenstein was initially suspicious of what she termed the "self-esteem evangelists," on the grounds that they both ignored the need for structural change and tended to "blame the victims" for the injuries caused to them by an unjust social system. But spending time with schoolgirls convinced her ". . . that the internal need not, and indeed should not, be ignored." Taking her approach to self-esteem in part from Morris Rosenberg, she summarizes her case:

> Girls with healthy self-esteem have an appropriate sense of their potential, their competence, and their innate value as individuals. They feel a sense of entitlement: license to take up space in the world, a right to be heard and to express the full spectrum of human emotions.[27]

If girls are to enter adulthood and realize their potential, Orenstein asserts, we must look at how we treat them and what we tell them, and see how it may damage or enhance their sense of self.

These feminist authors are fascinating conceptual entrepreneurs of self-esteem, in part because of the unlikelihood—evidenced by their own initial skepticism—of their working in such a capacity. It is arguable that both authors made a strategic decision to emphasize self-esteem, recognizing that the belief in self-esteem had become widespread and could therefore be useful to them in promoting and securing support for their analyses of gender discrimination against women. This seems a more plausible argument with respect to Orenstein than Steinem, who seems more deeply committed to the idea of self-esteem. Although Steinem's book is focused on self-esteem, Orenstein's is much less so—although she does begin with the results of the AAUW study and does highlight self-esteem as a crucial phenomenon.

However deeply committed these feminist writers are to the idea of self-esteem, one can argue that their discovery and promotion of self-esteem marked a new phase in the legitimacy of the myth of self-esteem. The California Task Force crystalized a widespread interest in and talk about self-esteem that had been growing throughout the 1980s. Indeed, it was probably the widespread publicity that was given to the Task Force that helped move discourse about self-esteem from the printed pages of magazines to the broadcast media to everyday conversation. But conceptual entrepreneurs need legitimacy as well as publicity, and for people sympathetic to the aims of feminism, Steinem and Orenstein could confer a legitimacy that the Task Force perhaps could not. Even those who would not consider themselves feminists would hear the discussion of issues of gender in terms of self-esteem and find evidence of their legitimacy in their very discussion by a well-known figure such as Steinem and sponsorship by the AAUW.

OVERCOMING THE PATHOLOGICAL CRITIC

Author-entrepreneurs have written a variety of books designed to provide specific methods for improving self-esteem. One of the best-selling of these is *Self-Esteem,* by Matthew McKay and Patrick Fanning.[28] First published in 1987, it had several printings, and the publisher issued a second edition in 1993. The book, which is written for the layperson but also addressed to professional therapists, emphasizes the application of cognitive behavioral therapy to self-esteem problems. Its goal, in other words, is to enable people to change the way they think about themselves and to find rewards in thinking positively rather than negatively.

"Self-esteem," the authors assert, "is essential for psychological survival."[29] Human beings, in their view, have a distinctive capacity for self-awareness that is our hallmark as a species but also a source of problems. We can be not only aware of ourselves, but also attach value to our identities, judge ourselves, and reject part of ourselves. The problem, they say, is that ". . . When you reject parts of yourself, you greatly damage the psychological structures that literally keep you alive."[30] Negative judgments of self, they say, lead to psychological pain, which in turn leads to the avoidance of anything that might cause this pain. Such avoidance makes people less likely to take risks, unwilling to meet new people, unable to be open with others, and less capable of expressing their sexuality.

People suffer from low self-esteem, the authors say, in part because of circumstances over which they have little control. Being overweight, being too short, and being the victim of poor parenting might well cause an individual to have low self-esteem, but there is little that can be done about many of these conditions. Moreover, although improving self-esteem might change some of the conditions of one's life, it will not alter some of the most important ones. The fact is, say the authors, self-esteem and circumstances are only "indirectly related." But there is good news: "There is another intervening factor that determines self-esteem 100% of the time: your thoughts."[31] The way people think about themselves determines their self-esteem. Hence, the authors make a powerful claim: "This book uses proven methods of cognitive behavioral therapy to raise your self-esteem by changing the way you interpret your life."[32]

The culprit responsible for low self-esteem is, say McKay and Fanning, the "pathological critic," which is the "negative inner voice that attacks and judges you."[33] The critic blames, compares, sets impossible standards, reminds us of failures, goads us to do our best, calls us names, exaggerates our weaknesses, and convinces us that others think we are terrible persons. The critic is always present and ready to wrongly interpret our actions. Everyone has such a critic, but those with low self-esteem have a "more vicious and vocal" one. In spite of being a source of great pain, this critic becomes an important part of the way people cope with the world, and so remains with them in spite of the psychological suffering.

The key to raising self-esteem is to overcome the critic, to learn to listen to one's own voice rather than the pathological critical voice. But to do this, the individual must learn to listen for and hear the critic, whose negative judgments are often hidden in the flow of the person's everyday internal monologue. The authors develop several exercises specifically to enable the individual to listen for and hear more clearly what the critic is saying. By writing down what the critic says, then exploring the ways in which they have become dependent upon this negative voice, people can learn alternative interpretations of their behavior. That is, they can learn to substitute their own interpretations for those of the critic.

Once attuned to the critic's judgments, the critic must be disarmed. The authors propose several methods for accomplishing this task. First, they propose, just as in everyday life we discount the activities or statements of others by uncovering their ulterior motives, we have to do this with the pathological critic. To disbelieve the critic's statements, we have to unmask the critic's motives. This can be accomplished by learning and using explicit verbal responses to the voice of the critic. One should say to the critic such things as, "You're slapping me around like my parents used to do, and I believe you because I believed them." "You're telling me they won't like me so that I won't be so hurt if I'm rejected."[34]

A second way to disarm the critic is to talk back. Methods for doing this include learning and reciting what the authors call "The Howitzer Mantras." "This is poison," one must say to the critic, "Stop it!" "No more put downs."[35] And one also must learn to recite affirmations of one's own worth. Believing strongly in the inherent worth of human beings regardless of what they do, the authors suggest specific affirmations: "I am worthwhile because I breathe and feel and am aware." "I feel pain, I love, I try to survive. I am a good person." Statements such as these answer the critic and, in doing so, counteract the critic's poison.

Third, the critic can be disarmed by being rendered useless. If the critic has become part of the person's psychological apparatus, then changes have to be made that will make the critic unnecessary. The authors suggest a variety of general ways in which this might be done, and the book is filled with specific exercises for accomplishing the goal. The individual should change his or her personal standards to fit the current situation, so he or she no longer feels obliged to live up to impossible standards. The individual should learn to see himself or herself more realistically rather than making comparisons with other people. The individual should cease making self-worth the motivation for success—instead, he or she should engage in activities for their intrinsic satisfaction. If accomplishment is worthwhile, it is for itself and not because it is necessary to validate one's own worth as a person. And the individual should learn self-acceptance, self-compassion, and self-forgiveness to control negative feelings.

Unlike a range of other self-esteem entrepreneurs whose focus is frequently on the consequences of high self-esteem, McKay and Fanning zero in on methods for improving self-esteem and have little to say about consequences. Self-esteem advocates, from positive thinkers to feminists, place a great deal of emphasis on the good individual results of high self-esteem. Positive thinkers regard self-esteem as a route to wealth and happiness. At least some feminists have come to define it as a measure of the damage done to women and as one means for their assertion of their rightful place in the world. And members of the National Association for Self-Esteem and their followers regard self-esteem not just as a good in itself but as a solution to social problems. But for McKay and Fanning, the good of self-esteem needs little justification; it is the method for finding it that needs attention.

This book's approach to self-esteem in some superficial way resembles the approach of the positive thinkers: to have self-esteem one must think positive thoughts about oneself. The cure for low self-esteem lies within the individual mind. But where the positive thinkers rely on exhortation and often religious inspiration, McKay and Fanning seek the legitimacy of an authorized and a reputable therapeutic method, "cognitive behavioral therapy." Theirs is a scientific language of rewards and punishments, of "proven methods" whereby the individual can shape his or her interpretation of self. Cognitive therapy has achieved great legitimacy, in fact, and it is acknowledged as one of the more effective methods for the treatment of disorders such as major depression. It is likely, then, that some of this legitimacy rubs off on the self-esteem movement as well as on McKay and Fanning's book. Their approach also has much in common with humanistic psychology, in the sense that it emphasizes self-acceptance. Yet, again, cognitive therapy may have an edge over humanistic psychology, especially in its more "New Age" manifestations, with respect to legitimacy.

RAISING "SELF-ESTEEMING" KIDS

If self-esteem is important for adults, it also is important for children. Indeed, if much of what adults must do for themselves is overcome the damage to their self-esteem suffered in childhood, then it becomes especially important for them to avoid their own parents' mistakes. Not surprisingly, parents can find help in this task, not only in the pages of *Parents' Magazine* but in books devoted to the topic. One of these, *Raising Your Child's Inner Self-Esteem,* by Karen Owens, develops a revealing take on the work parents must do. It celebrates the usual virtues of high self-esteem, arguing that "healthy self-esteem" is essential for a healthy child, because self-esteem is a "basic need for every human being."[36] But it distinguishes between "outer" and "inner" self-esteem, emphasizing the latter in its advice as well as in its title.

Outer self-esteem, says Owens, depends upon the judgments of others. Mentioning Charles Horton Cooley (who was demoted from his status as a founder of American sociology to a "self-esteem expert") and his "looking-glass self," she points out that young children derive most of their self-esteem from external sources. "During these early years," she argues, "children need positive feedback from parents and thrive on arbitrary praise and approval bestowed on them by their parents."[37] The young child has a strong need for unconditional positive regard and is strongly oriented to his or her perceptions of the judgments of others.

Outer self-esteem is not enough, the author claims. Criticizing the self-esteem movement for putting too much emphasis on the judgments of others as the basis for self-image, she defines inner self-esteem as based on *self-evaluations.* "Inner self-esteem," she writes, "is not given to children by others, but is earned through children's developing competent behaviors and skills in socially valued areas." Although the standards of judgment the child must meet are socially defined, the individual is the final arbiter of inner self-esteem. Children must develop a sense that they are in control, that the sense of accomplishment they derive from doing well in school, for example, is not dependent on the arbitrary praise of parents or teachers, but on their own recognition of their success.

To make outer self-esteem the most important goal, argues Owens, is not only to paint a "passive and conforming" portrait of human beings, but also to produce children who are too geared to the expectations of others. Children with healthy inner self-esteem, she writes, are "not constantly worrying about how they measure up in comparison to others" and they "do not need constant praise from others" to maintain their self-esteem. The child dependent upon external sources for self-esteem develops an "ingrowing" mind, focused on maintaining old positive impressions of the self and limiting new information to that which supports an existing self-image. The child with high inner self-esteem develops an "outgrowing" mind, one capable of thinking flexibly and capable of new experience.

Inner self-esteem, which is "earned" and dependent upon "actual behavior and real accomplishments," becomes more important as the child grows older. The developmental tasks of infancy are the development of attachment to and trust in parents, and these cannot be made conditional on the infant's behavior. During infancy and early childhood, the child must have the sense that he or she is unconditionally loved and accepted. Accordingly, it is necessary to bestow praise on the child, to be accepting of the child's individual temperament, and to do whatever it takes to create a sense of security.

As the child grows, however, there are additional developmental tasks. During early childhood, the child must develop a sense of self-sufficiency, independence, and autonomy. Later, during middle childhood, the focus turns to school success and getting along with peers. For adolescents, the tasks include further developing a sense of autonomy while maintaining a connection with parents. Or, as other child development specialists might put it, the task is one of identity formation. At each stage, the development of self-esteem is dependent upon the successful mastery of these developmental tasks.

The role of the parents is to do the right thing at each stage, to maximize the likelihood of this occurring. During infancy, the parents must be "sensitive" and "nurturing" and responsive to children's signals. During early childhood, they must "recognize and accept the child's temperament" and "help the child feel protected and safe." In middle childhood, parents must "teach effective communication skills," "have realistic expectations," "help the child with homework," and "believe that their child is capable of succeeding." And during adolescence, they must be "authoritative, not authoritarian or permissive," "warm," and "firm but fair."[38]

This approach to parenting has a number of characteristics that deserve comment. First, like McKay and Fanning, Owens proposes no easy route to high self-esteem. These authors clearly profit from the sales of their books, but they do not promote the idea that self-esteem can be had quickly or cheaply. Although McKay and Fanning say thoughts control self-esteem, it takes work to get one's thoughts in order. Owens clearly constructs parents as being capable of ensuring their children's self-esteem if they follow correct procedures, but they must actually do the right thing. In contrast, much of the slickly packaged self-esteem material available on the market seems to propose a less bumpy and faster route.

Second, the sharp contrast between outer and inner self-esteem that Owens draws is not only an integral part of her conception of the nature of self-esteem but also a signal that here may lie an important issue for the proponents and opponents of self-esteem. The question of the sources of self-esteem—whether the surrounding social world or the individual's own judgment—seems to be a crucial one for this author. Moreover, even though she emphasizes inner self-esteem, she walks a fine line between contending points of view. Self-esteem is earned on the basis of real accomplishment, but in the early years at least it rests on unconditional acceptance. The individual must feel that he or she is the final judge of the accomplishments on which self-regard is based, but the standards themselves are derived from society.

Finally, the advice Owens provides to parents strikes one as so reasonable, as being fully in accord with the "common sense" one develops as a parent. It would, in fact, have this quality of reasonableness even if self-esteem were not mentioned in the book. What the author prescribes as methods for building self-esteem in children could well be prescribed more generally and simply as methods for being a "good enough" parent. I make this judgment neither as praise nor criticism, however. Rather, it suggests to me that her book is indeed "authoritative," not in the scientific sense, which I suspect she means, but in a cultural sense. The book is a *culturally* authoritative prescription for raising an American child.[39] If it is, then the author's distinction between inner and outer self-esteem and the fine line she walks between the society and the individual tells us something important about this culture. I will explore this issue further in later chapters.

TEACHING SELF-ESTEEM

The topic of children brings us finally to an arena where self-esteem has found its most successful entrepreneurs and by far its best market: education. Self-esteem has taken a place alongside reading, writing, and arithmetic as a major goal of education. Indeed, critics argue that it has supplanted academic concerns and is at least partially responsible for a perceived decline in academic standards. Because it is so prominent there, self-esteem in the schools deserves a lengthy discussion in its own chapter. And that discussion, we will see, provides a good starting place for an interpretation of the social and cultural significance of self-esteem.

NOTES

1. Howard S. Becker, *Outsiders.* New York: Free Press, 1963.
2. See Malcolm Spector and John I. Kitsuse, *Constructing Social Problems,* Rev. Ed. New York: Aldine de Gruyter, 1987.
3. Source: On-line versions of ERIC (time periods reflect the organization of the databases); Psychinfo; Infotrak; and catalog of The W. E. B. Dubois Library of the University of Massachusetts at Amherst.

4. Joan Costello, "The Sensitive Years." *Parents' Magazine* 59, February 1984: 100.
5. Anne C. Bernstein, "Feeling Great (About Myself): How Can You Help Your Child Feel Self-Confident And Resilient?" *Parents' Magazine* 57, September 1982: 56.
6. Paul Chance, "Your Child's Self-Esteem." *Parents' Magazine* 57, January 1982: 59.
7. Bernstein, op. cit., 51.
8. James P. Comer, "Encouraging Self-Esteem." *Parents' Magazine* 62, February 1987: 162.
9. Jolene Brown, "How to Rekindle Confidence and Esteem." *Successful Farming* 84, March 1986: 11.
10. George C. Thornton, "Borrower's Net Worth Depends on Self-worth." *ABA Banking Journal* 75, October 1983: 166.
11. Brian S. Tracey, "I Can't, I Can't: How Self-Concept Shapes Performance." *Management World* 15, April–May 1986: 8.
12. Pete Bradshaw and Sandra Shullman, "Managing High-tech Employees through Self-Esteem." *Infosystems* 30, March 1983: 98.
13. Barbara Finney, "Writing for Fun: A Magical Jar of Self-Esteem." *Writer's Digest* 67, June 1987: 35.
14. Shad Helmstetter, *What to Say When You Talk to Yourself* (New York: MJF Books, 1986); *Predictive Parenting: What to Say When You Talk to Your Kids* (New York: Morrow, 1989); *You Can Excel in Times of Change* (New York: Pocket Books, 1991); *Finding the Fountain of Youth Inside Yourself* (New York: Pocket Books, 1990); *Choices* (New York: Pocket Books, 1989); *The Self-Talk Solution* (New York: W. Morrow, 1987). Helmstetter maintains a home page on the World Wide Web. URL: http://www.monsoon.org/selftalk/index.html.
15. See Robert A. Schuller, "The Theology of Self-Esteem." *Saturday Evening Post* 252, May–June 1980: 42ff. Also see V. Gilbert Baars, Kenneth S. Kantzer, and David F. Wells, "Hard Questions for Robert Schuller about Sin and Self-Esteem." *Christianity Today* 28, August 10, 1984: 14ff.
16. Darla Walker, "Women and Self-Esteem." URL: http://www.crusade.org/wto/esteem/esteem.html. Document revised September 15, 1995.
17. John Vasconcellos, "Preface," in *The Social Importance of Self-Esteem*, eds. Andrew M. Mecca, Neil J. Smelser, and John Vasconcellos. Berkeley: University of California Press, 1989, xii.
18. Ibid.
19. Ibid.
20. Ibid., xiii.
21. Neil J. Smelser, "Self-Esteem and Social Problems: An Introduction,"

in *The Social Importance of Self-Esteem.* Berkeley: University of California Press, 1989:15.

22. *Time* magazine, "Learning Self-Esteem," 135. January 29, 1990: 29.

23. *Christian Science Monitor,* "California Esteemin' " (Editorial) 82, February 14, 1990: 20.

24. *Self-Esteem Today* (the newsletter of the National Association for Self-Esteem), Vol. 8, Fall 1995, 21.

25. Gloria Steinem, *Revolution From Within: A Book of Self-Esteem.* Boston: Little-Brown, 1992, 25.

26. Ibid., 33.

27. Peggy Orenstein, *Schoolgirls: Young Women, Self-Esteem, and the Confidence Gap.* New York: Doubleday, 1994, xix.

28. Matthew McKay and Patrick Fanning, *Self-Esteem.* Oakland, California: New Harbinger Publications, 1987; Second edition, 1993. My discussion is based on the first edition.

29. Ibid., 1.

30. Ibid.

31. Ibid., 3.

32. Ibid.

33. Ibid., 15.

34. Ibid., 33.

35. Ibid., 34.

36. Karen Owens, *Raising Your Child's Inner Self-Esteem: The Authoritative Guide from Infancy through the Teen Years.* New York: Plenum Press, 1995, 1.

37. Ibid., 4.

38. Quoted material is from ibid., chapter summaries on pp. 46, 72, 112, 142, and 183.

39. It might be more precise to say the book is an authoritative middle-class prescription for child rearing. In a society in which the vast majority consider themselves members of the middle class, this is not much of a qualification. Even though upper-class and working-class Americans may not necessarily share middle-class views, these are the views that are widely promulgated and presented as authoritative. Likewise, there are ethnic differences in child-rearing preferences, but even in a supposedly "multicultural" society, the views of child-rearing experts are privileged.

4

———

Self-Esteem Goes to School

———

The contemporary visibility of self-esteem is due in good part to the successful promotion of this concept by educational theorists and its enthusiastic adoption by classroom teachers. Education is an appropriate arena, therefore, in which to search for a deeper understanding of the myth of self-esteem. In the pages of educational manuals and textbooks and in countless classrooms, teachers fervently and repeatedly invoke the myth of self-esteem. The social practices to which the myth gives rise themselves reaffirm the myth, as teachers help create the very psychological reality they believe to be a natural part of the human condition.

The first task in exploring the uses of the myth in education is to distill from contemporary educational literature the basic premises of the educational theory of self-esteem. Having done this, I will examine in more detail a few of the classroom practices to which this theory gives rise. Finally, I will develop several interpretations of its social significance.

THE EDUCATIONAL THEORY
OF SELF-ESTEEM

Over the past quarter-century, the view that self-esteem is a crucial prerequisite to learning has come to lie at the center of much educational thinking. A great many books urge teachers to take at least partial responsibility for their students' self-esteem and recommend specific techniques designed to enable them to meet this professional obligation. One popular book, *100 Ways to Enhance Self-Concept in the Classroom*, for example, provides detailed instructions for classroom exercises and activities that supposedly support and improve students' self-esteem.[1] Magazines and journals that offer practical advice to teachers frequently publish articles that recount the specific techniques and usually the successes of various programs founded on this premise.

One book aimed at teachers, *The Six Vital Ingredients of Self-Esteem: How to Develop Them in Your Students*, by Bettie B. Youngs, provides a typical version of self-esteem theory and explains why teachers are so important. Self-esteem, according to Dr. Youngs, is ". . . the esteem you hold for you, the value you place on your personhood." People who place more value on themselves, she asserts, are more self-confident, achieve more, take risks more willingly, and are more likely to attain their goals. According to the author, more and more children are "at risk" in contemporary society, not only for academic failure but also for ". . . drug involvement, youth pregnancy; dropping out of school, disrespect for educators, parents, and fellow students, and apathy and boredom, and other such maladies." Educators are important because they can make a difference—and sometimes they are the only ones who will make a difference—in helping children overcome the difficulties that beset them and learn to value themselves. It is the educator's role ". . . to empower our students. We do this by helping students believe in themselves." The educator must and can ". . . create a classroom environment where students can develop high self-esteem."[2]

Teachers and educational theorists hold such a great variety of views on the importance of self-esteem and how to encourage it that it is difficult to summarize them and perhaps impossible to do so in a way that does not distort the views of one or another proponent. Still, to get a handle on the myth of self-esteem in schools we must somehow capture this diversity and distill it into a theory of self-esteem with which supporters of this approach to education would likely agree in general principle, if not in every detail. At least four basic ideas form the foundation of such a theory.

First, there is broad agreement that self-esteem is a matter of right, something to which the child (and every human being) is entitled, which need not be earned or justified. Children simply have an unqualified right to feel good about themselves, and these self-feelings are as important a goal of teaching as any other educational outcome. One psychologist and radio personality put it simply in the following terms: "All children are created worthy and are due the right to personal respect and dignity."[3] Sometimes self-esteem is seen as an entitlement because it is a fundamental human need:

> Positive self-esteem is a basic need for every human being.
> Just as the body needs nutritious food to be healthy, so the
> personality needs esteem from others and from self to
> achieve emotional health.[4]

In addition to such clear assertions of self-esteem as a matter of right, the idea that self-esteem is an entitlement lies implicit in many discussions of self-esteem, especially through the familiar concept of "self-acceptance."

Advice-givers assert that the basis for self-esteem lies partly in people's capacity to accept themselves for who or what they are:

> When we accept ourselves we also respect ourselves ...[5]

> Respect is shown when children receive recognition for who they are and what they do.[6]

In other words, children should not unduly try to meet the expectations of others, define themselves in ways others impose, or judge themselves too harshly for their failings. They are entitled to self-esteem, regardless of who they are, what they do, or how others view them.

Moreover, the same web of implication that makes self-esteem an individual entitlement also defines its maintenance and enhancement as an *obligation* of parents and teachers. Self-esteem is portrayed not only as something one secures for oneself but also as something that significant others should bestow. One professor of education, arguing that self-respect empowers the child, puts it this way:

> Teachers can play a pivotal role in building children's respect for themselves ... the power of a teacher to breathe new life into children and empower them for all time is awesome.[7]

Parents also are obligated to involve themselves in their children's schooling in order to foster a better self-image. When a child is not doing well in school,

> The child's self-image is the first area that needs attention. Don't be afraid to tell your child over and over again how bright and talented he or she is.[8]

In word and deed, it appears, the adult world is obligated to maintain and, where possible, enhance the child's self-esteem.

Second, self-esteem can be taught. The educational theory of self-esteem stresses that teachers can directly influence the self-esteem of their pupils through methods that can themselves be taught to teachers. One author, a clinical psychologist, describes seven "secrets" for developing self-esteem in children. Teachers should try to create situations where "failure is unlikely," so success and the self-esteem that comes with it are virtually assured. Teachers should acknowledge the positive contributions of their students, because doing so "nurtures success." Teachers should "capitalize on success" by helping children succeed at further activities in areas where they have already been successful. They also should keep expectations realistic, so children with low self-esteem do not become overly anxious and thus too eager to please others but less likely to do so. And teachers should not be boring, because "boredom depresses self-esteem."[9] Another book devoted to instructing teachers on how to improve students' self-esteem takes a broader view, arguing that self-esteem is founded on the six vital ingredients of physical safety, emotional security, identity, affiliation, competence, and mission, all of which the teacher can influence.[10]

Third, self-esteem must be taught in the schools because so many children come to school with damaged self-esteem and because their self-esteem continues to be threatened, both inside the school and outside of it. There is, in the words of one educational textbook, an "epidemic of inferiority."[11] Children come to school with self-esteem that has been wounded by faulty parenting, unfair standards of evaluation in the home and in society at large, and prejudice and discrimination on the basis of race, ethnicity, and social class. It is the school's responsibility to help repair this damage and prevent it from worsening. This must be done not only in the interest of academic success but also for the child's overall well-being and happiness.

Educators' discourse of self-esteem formulates a critique, albeit a weak one, of the competitive individualism that in their view mars the society and damages children. The critique is epitomized by the words of a psychologist who, after portraying two fictional children with poor self-images, one a slow-learning boy and the other an overweight girl, explains their victimization as a result of erroneous societal standards of evaluation and the denial of worth to some children. The problem is that

> we reserve praise and admiration for the few who have been blessed from birth with the characteristics we, wrongly, value most highly—beauty, brains, and riches. It is a vicious system, and we must counterbalance its impact by helping young people develop self-esteem.[12]

Although, the author asserts, parents are obliged to help their children compete in a world of competitive individualism that enforces such false standards, they have other obligations:

> . . . while helping my child to compete, I also instruct him on the true values of life: love for mankind, integrity, truthfulness, and devotion to God.[13]

The opposition to competitiveness and evaluation based on achievement, is a corollary to the belief in entitlement. To say that all deserve self-esteem is also to say that some are denied it because it is based on standards of achievement they cannot or should not be asked to meet.

Educators who subscribe to the self-esteem theory seek to convince not only other educators that the self-esteem of their students is at risk, but also the students themselves. In one exercise, recommended by the authors of *100 Ways*, known as "IALAC," the teacher tells a story to graphically illustrate attacks on a hypothetical child's self-esteem.[14] The teacher writes the letters IALAC in large print on a sheet of paper, holding it up and explaining that the letters stand for "I am lovable and capable." "Everyone," the teacher explains, "carries an invisible IALAC sign around with them at all times and wherever they go." This sign represents how the child feels about himself or herself, and its size is affected by the treatment the child receives from others. Each time the child is put down or is the target of rejection or nastiness, a piece of the IALAC sign is destroyed. The teacher illustrates this idea by telling a story about a child whose sign is progressively destroyed because he is called lazy and forgetful, chosen last to play ball at recess, given a low grade on a test, and forced to endure other negative experiences. As the teacher describes each negative event, he or she rips off a piece of the IALAC sign. When the story is finished, the teacher leads the class in a discussion, asking them to focus on what tears up their signs, how they feel when their signs are ripped up, and how they can help people enlarge their signs rather than destroy them. Teachers as well as students must learn that self-esteem is at risk and that efforts must be undertaken to bolster and improve it.

Fourth, self-esteem is regarded as a precondition to learning, the psychological attribute upon which the success of schooling depends. As one author expresses it in an account of a high school designed to foster "achievement through self-esteem" for students who have not succeeded in a traditional high school, "At Apollo [High School], our goal is to increase students' self-esteem, in the belief that self-esteem produces achievement."[15] An Alabama school teacher asserts that, "Elementary schools need to get kids off on the right foot, and self-esteem is absolutely fundamental to school success."[16] Children who do not feel good about themselves will not be motivated to learn, it is argued, nor will they be able to participate in social relationships with teachers and other children that are conducive to learning. They will lack confidence in themselves and be unable to see themselves as successful learners. And they will likely disrupt the classroom and thus the learning of others. In contrast, the child who feels good about himself or herself will want to learn and will be able to do so, and it does not matter how this self-esteem developed. Although educational successes will promote self-esteem and thus further learning, self-esteem by itself will promote success and learning even if it does not originate in educational success. In other words, self-esteem both follows and precedes successful learning.

Why is self-esteem held as a prerequisite to learning? Educationists' views on this question run the gamut from analyses carefully grounded in social and behavioral research and theory to muddy intellectual stews composed of wildly disparate ingredients. Some accounts stress the complex interdependence of self-esteem and achievement, where growth in one both stimulates and depends upon the development of the other. Other accounts give full causal priority to self-esteem itself, arguing that self-esteem will dramatically improve the child's capacity to learn, no matter how it is fostered. In general, children with higher self-esteem are said to feel more confident or "empowered," to relate better to others, but at the same time to be less anxious about pleasing others, to perform tasks better because they *believe* they can do so, and to be generally more constructive, optimistic, and involved in life. All of the themes we have already experienced—from positive thinking to inner self-esteem—are encountered in one or another version of educational theory.

THE TEACHING OF SELF-ESTEEM

Adherents of the self-esteem theory believe that the self-esteem of significant numbers of students must be raised and that it can be raised through the application of proper techniques. Although accounts describe a wide range of such techniques, they seem to fall into three general categories.

First, the emphasis on self-esteem as an entitlement leads to efforts to get teachers to accept children for who and what they are and to encourage children to do the same. This approach frequently leads to an emphasis on group identity as a source of individual self-esteem. Because accounts of the prevalence of low self-esteem often are grounded in theories of racism, classism, or sexism, it is not surprising to find considerable emphasis on techniques to counter these forces. A Michigan City, Indiana, fifth-grade teacher, for example, makes what she calls "pride" a continuing theme of her work in the classroom. Because many of her students are poor, single-parent, latchkey children who compare themselves unfavorably to middle-class standards of worth, she tries to ward off the denigrations of race and class by instilling "pride" in social origins. She tells stories of her own experiences as a child of immigrant parents and gives special support to children whose different ethnic backgrounds are criticized by other children.

> Make pride the continuing classroom campaign it deserves
> to be. . . . Because no matter what economic, social, or
> racial group you deal with, children need your encourage-
> ment. It is up to each of us to teach pride.[17]

This teacher also argues that in spite of the school's emphasis on academic achievement as a basis for self-esteem, many children will not do well in school. So, she says, ". . . as teachers we have to offer children other means to achieve, other ways to feel good about themselves."[18] Techniques such as these are designed to counter denigrations of self-esteem based in part on race or ethnicity, gender, and social class by focusing positive attention on these social roles and group affiliations, as well as upon the individual's intrinsic worth.

The explicit anchoring of self-esteem in group affiliation is even more strongly evident in current Afro-centric and multicultural theories of education. An *Essence* magazine article encourages parents to support the establishment of Afro-centric curricula in schools and quotes a leading proponent of Afro-centrism, Molefi Kete Asante:

> All children must be centered in a historical place, or their self-esteem suffers. Our students have been moved to the margins of the educational experience.[19]

Asante argues that the "Eurocentric" curriculum is damaging, indeed devastating to the black child's sense of self. Although perhaps most strongly expressed in the Afro-centric movement, a belief that ethnic pride fosters individual self-esteem also is expressed by others, who argue that self-esteem is undermined by the stress of urban life, ethnics' sense of exclusion from the system, and stereotypes propagated by the mass media.[20]

Proponents of the self-esteem theory in education have created an amazing variety of classroom exercises to encourage children to accept themselves for what they are. In one of these exercises, recommended by the authors of *100 Ways,* the teacher is shown a technique for getting children to express love for themselves. The structure of the exercise is simple. The teacher dictates the beginnings of several sentences to the children, who must then complete each sentence with a self-accepting or self-affirming statement. The teacher dictates such beginnings as "I love myself because," "I love myself even though," "Yes, I love myself even though I sometimes," "It's not so bad to," and "I forgive myself for." The underlying theory of the exercise is that children have to be given permission to express love for themselves and, in fact, taught to do so. In the view of the authors, ". . . acceptance *by* ourselves *of* ourselves as we are, with all our failings, warts, occasional stupid behaviors, and faults, is the first step toward good mental health."[21]

Another exercise attempts to teach students to deal with "those nasty putdowns" that are commonplace in childhood. "Ugly remarks and nicknames directed at a child by siblings or peers is one of the most damaging and persistent occurrences of childhood," the authors write. Teachers are instructed to write a phrase—*NO MATTER WHAT YOU SAY OR DO TO ME, I AM STILL A WORTHWHILE PERSON*—on the blackboard and have the class copy it several times. Then, the teacher insults the class in a good-natured way, and the class responds to each insult by repeating the phrase in chorus. The object, the authors say, is to teach the child to internalize this phrase as a habitual response to derogation, thus maintaining a sense of self-worth in the face of attacks on it.[22]

Teachers also work to bolster individual self-esteem by making the individual the object of pride. One teacher does so by means of a "Pride Month," during which students and teachers engage in special activities. The Pride Month is divided into four week-long segments: Pride in Self, School Pride, Community Pride, and National Pride. During Pride in Self Week, which focuses attention specifically on the individual child, special activities include creating personal booklets, presenting hobbies, hosting parent visits, and dressing up to look one's best. During this week, ". . . students (and teachers, too) take a closer look at themselves. It is a get-better-acquainted-and-feel-good-about-yourself week."[23] The personal booklets created by the students include pages on which they place pictures of themselves, information about themselves and their lives, information about their families gained from interviews, and a personal "coat of arms."

"Self-acceptance" thus seems to come in both individual and group varieties. On the one hand, this phrase refers to the desire of individuals to be accepted by others, to receive from them the words or sympathy or praise that will bolster self-esteem. Whatever the individual child's failings, according to this point of view, he or she is entitled to self-esteem and must be taught not only this fact but ways of remembering it and defending it from attack by others. On the other hand, the phrase also refers to the obstacles placed in the way of self-acceptance by society, and its devaluation or marginalization of certain groups. From this perspective, self-esteem is still an individual right, but it is something withheld from the child because of his or her membership in a group, and it can only be restored by identification with that group.

This contrast is worth noting because it points to the differing uses that can be made of a single word. Individual self-acceptance—"Accept me for *what* I am!"—tends to emphasize the centrality of the individual and thus to loosen the bonds of social control, because it argues that self-worth should not be tied to one's performance in school or to behavior on the playground or at home. Self-esteem is something one deserves, regardless. Collective self-acceptance—"Accept me for *who* I am!"—ties the person to the group and its claims, for to have self-esteem one must accept group membership, learn about the group, and identify oneself with it. Attitudes toward social life expressed in these two uses of the word *self-esteem* are thus in a sense miles apart. The former mirrors individualism, stressing the inner life of the individual and regarding the social world as a possible impediment to the expression of the self. The latter, by anchoring self-esteem in allegiance to the group and its standards, seems to oppose individualism. Self-esteem appears to have quite divergent meanings, then, bringing together under one apparent conceptual umbrella people whose social attitudes and goals are actually quite different.

The second broad approach to building self-esteem focuses on the classroom itself, particularly on the ways in which teachers can foster self-esteem by creating success. In one typical article by a clinical psychologist disclosing several "secrets for building kids' self-esteem" to readers of *Instructor*, teachers are urged to "build in success" by creating situations where "failure is unlikely."

> Success builds self-esteem, especially when the chain of successes remains continuous and unbroken.[24]

Teachers should "capitalize on success" whenever they see it; they should be sure to "value and acknowledge" a child's successes; and they should "keep expectations realistic." One finds few explicit arguments that academic standards should be drastically lowered, but there is an implication that maintaining high standards is secondary to the task of fostering self-esteem and thereby enabling the child to meet such standards later on.

"*Feeling* capable," as one author puts it, "is the forerunner to *being* capable."[25] Given this premise, the teacher's task is to help students develop the feeling that they are capable. One way to do so, they are advised, is to "build on the positive." The teacher should praise the child's effort and find positive things to say about the child's work, calling attention to the child's good work and good behavior. Praise should be personal—it is most effective when shared "heart-to-heart" with the student. Praise also should be given immediately, only when deserved, and should be specific and consistent. The teacher should criticize the behavior and not the child, for to label the child "stupid" or "irresponsible" not only encourages him or her to "tune out" but also prevents a sense of capability from developing.

A third set of techniques emphasizes the need to pay attention to the individual child, to respect and make the child feel important and special. As one proponent of self-esteem put it,

> To help students build their self-esteem, Apollo staff provide them with the four A's: Attention, Acceptance, Appreciation, and Affection.[26]

An elementary school teacher in Auburn, Alabama, attempts to boost self-esteem through her "VIP-for-a-week project," which each week makes a single child the focus of attention, special activities, parental visits, and other activities designed to make him or her feel special, valued, and important. Such efforts rest on the view that the child should be valued, appreciated, the focus of warm and supportive attention, and, in the words of one professor of education, *respected*.

> If we think about our own teachers—particularly those
> who have been powerful forces in shaping us as adults—
> we remember how they empowered us. They *respected* us.
> They seemed to understand how we felt. They recognized
> and appreciated who we were and what we did. They
> asked for our ideas and listened to them with serious
> consideration. They increased rather than crushed our
> choices. They asked for our opinions and they used them
> in making important decisions about what was happen-
> ing in class. When such respect is shown for children, self-
> respect grows.[27]

Attention and respect build self-esteem, it is argued, and so enable the child
to be successful in school and later on in life.

One author argues that an effective way to develop students' sense of
uniqueness or being special is to display awareness of ". . . what is going on
in their emotional lives, such as when we acknowledge that they are in a
good or bad mood."[28] Planning tests around major events in students' lives,
such as athletic contests, and giving students choices about their work also
convey to them a sense that they count. Teachers should also tell their students that they are special and that they enjoy teaching them and "go the
extra mile in helping them with their work."

REALIZING INDIVIDUALISM

The beliefs and practices associated with the self-esteem theory of education have a variety of consequences. First, and perhaps of greatest significance, they help realize the very culture of individualism that gives rise to
them in the first place. Ideas about the existence of a true self, the importance of recognition and acceptance, and the centrality of the person to
which we referred in Chapter 2 become translated into specific beliefs and
practices in the world of education. These beliefs and practices, in turn, give
renewed life and credibility to the very ideas that spawned them. To understand how the myth of self-esteem functions, we must grasp this process of
realization, in which myths not only take hold of our perception of the
world but also shape its reality.

The idea of cultural realization is quite simple, but nonetheless important. Human beings see the world through lenses that have been ground for
them by the cultures in which they participate; they seek goals that have
been set for them; and they generally travel along well-established paths to
reach them. As a result, they act in ways that realize—that is, make real—the
culture that has nourished and shaped them. Their actions, based on cul-

tural beliefs, bring the culture to life. If they believe in the existence of God, for example, they will look for signs of divine intervention in or relevance to their lives. They will engage in activities that they have been taught are essential in order to make their living, please God, or attain salvation—or whatever it is their religious beliefs direct them to seek. What human beings look for they tend to find, particularly when almost anything can be interpreted as meeting their expectations. If one is looking for a divine presence or intervention, it is not difficult to perceive it, since almost any natural event or human act can be interpreted as such evidence. If, for example, like some early Protestants, one thinks worldly success is a sign that one is predestined for salvation, one can cling to this belief in part because there is little that can disconfirm it. One only knows with certainty if one is saved when one dies. Some kinds of beliefs, then, tend to confirm themselves, because they lead us to see events in ways that support them. Various practical actions have the same effect: If one believes that in order to grow crops one must present the gods with sacrifices, then one will probably do so. If the crops grow, the efficacy of the sacrifice is confirmed. If the crops do not grow, the belief in sacrifices is likely to persist, for it is easy to imagine that one did not properly perform the sacrifices.

More subtly, culture tends to produce human beings who have the goals, skills, motives, knowledge, and other attributes that are necessary for acting in terms of its beliefs and carrying out its practices. These same skills and knowledge also may make it difficult or impossible for them to act in any other way. People who believe in gods or God, or those who practice animal sacrifice, read from the Torah, or take Holy Communion, organize their daily activities and indeed their lives in ways that make it possible to sustain these beliefs and engage in these activities. They learn about the ways of the gods, how to read from the Torah scroll, or how to accept the Host from the priest. They believe they must say their prayers or confess their sins if they are to be received in heaven in a state of grace, and they become anxious if they are unable to do these things. They explain their actions by citing religious motives, take pride in their mastery of theology, and teach others how to achieve whatever it is their religion teaches them to seek. In short, they become people who are psychologically immersed in their culture and its beliefs and practices, who can extricate themselves from it only with difficulty, if at all.

In a similar way, the particular beliefs and practices associated with the self-esteem theory of education tend to confirm the more general and widespread idea that there is some such thing as the self that merits attention and care, that individuals deserve and need recognition and acceptance if the self is to be enhanced, and that the individual is the most important unit in the world. The beliefs and practices discussed earlier arise out of this general framework of ideas. Practitioners—both classroom teachers and those who teach teachers—take this general framework for granted as truth, and they create beliefs and practices that are consistent with it. By expounding their beliefs and engaging in their practices, they reaffirm the more general ideas on which they are founded. Moreover, the practices of teachers tend to produce students who, in at least some ways, look and act like what the theories say they should look and act like. They tend to act as though they believe they have worthy and good inner essences, regardless of what people say or how they behave, that they deserve recognition and attention from others, and that their unique individual needs should be considered first and foremost.

How and why does this cultural realization occur? First, the ideas and practices of self-esteem theorists provide ways for people to focus on themselves and believe in the reality of the "self" and "self-esteem." Each of the many techniques educators and classroom teachers have worked out for the enhancement of self-esteem is a way of experiencing the self. Many contemporary social psychologists would argue that the reality of the self lies in the performances people give and the contexts in which they think about themselves or are provided with information about themselves. From this perspective, each classroom exercise is a social context in which children "perform" selves or provide intimate information to themselves or others. From the perspective of the teachers and children, of course, these are techniques for discovering or enhancing the self, which they often believe is already there and needs only to be discovered or protected. But from the more skeptical viewpoint of the social psychologist, we can regard these techniques *as* the self. That is, people have selves to the extent and in the ways that a culture makes it possible for them to do so, and what the educational theory of self-esteem has done is to provide a particular set of ways of having and experiencing the self.

Moreover, these techniques not only create the self and make it important, but at the same time provide scientific legitimacy for doing so. The child—indeed, anyone who subscribes to the self-esteem theory—is encouraged to believe that it is acceptable and desirable to be preoccupied with oneself, praise oneself, dissociate self-esteem from behavior or group memberships, and regard acceptance by self and others as a basic human need. At least within those social contexts controlled or influenced by the school and by teachers who believe in the theory of self-esteem, preoccupation with the self becomes a legitimate and perhaps even an obligatory idea. That is, whatever natural tendency the child may have to be self-centered or self-preoccupied, such exercises make this inclination seem quite appropriate, and to some extent they *demand* such activities from the child.

One can imagine third graders, for example, searching their minds for ideas with which to complete the sentence, "Yes, I love myself even though I sometimes. . . ." and feeling a powerful sense of obligation to do so. From the child's vantage point, the activity is part of the definition of what school is and what it is for. It helps define what people are like and how they should experience and describe themselves. And crucially, such activities take on a normative character, for given the emotional power of the teacher and the pressure from other children, it becomes not merely routine to inspect and reveal the self, not merely appropriate, but obligatory.

Such social practices, which legitimate and demand self-revelation, are not without ironies, two of which deserve particular mention here. First, teachers who use such procedures in the classroom, along with those who teach them to use them, no doubt regard the exercises as being in the best interest of their students. Indeed, they would argue that enhancing the self-esteem of their students is, in fact, "empowering," something that increases the child's capacity to make good choices, to be autonomous and in charge of the self, and to succeed. Yet from a more skeptical perspective, these exercises are subtle instruments of social control. The child *must* be taught to like himself or herself. He or she *must* be made conscious of the variety of ways in which the self may come under attack. The child *must* confess self-doubt or self-loathing, bringing into light the feelings that he or she might well prefer to keep private. The child *must* take the teacher's attitude toward himself or herself—"I am somebody!" "I am capable and loving!"—regardless of what the child thinks. He or she *must* learn that there are acceptable and unacceptable ways of thinking about oneself, and that it is best to display acceptable ways. These practices in some ways are not unlike those of the early Puritans, who were convinced of the utter sinfulness of human beings and pressured themselves and their children to confess their sins and recognize that they were rotten and sinful to the core.

I do not wish to overstate this line of criticism, for children's self-esteem is probably not nearly as susceptible to improvement (or damage) by teachers as the latter are led to believe. The contemporary school is nowhere near as powerful an agency of social control as the Puritan community. Moreover, few people—myself included—would argue that it would be better if children were encouraged to feel badly about themselves. But it is worth considering that beliefs about self-esteem and practices for enhancing it have a darker side associated with controlling rather than liberating the person. Even if such exercises do not raise self-esteem, they provide the child with definitions of what he or she is supposed to feel, as well as methods for bringing self-feelings in line with expectations.

The second irony is that in arguing for such techniques, educators often decry the extreme difficulty they feel Americans have in expressing pride in themselves or in accepting the idea that they can love themselves. The irony lies in the fact that by far the dominant mode of social criticism in the United States over the last two or three decades has taken the exact opposite point of view, arguing that Americans are far too self-preoccupied,

too individualistic, too inclined to "look out for number one."[29] It is difficult to generalize about the ease or difficulty with which various groups in
a culturally diverse society either express or conceal pride or satisfaction in
themselves. On the whole, however, American cultural values favor the
individual and, while making humility a virtue, make pride a greater one.
Thus, educators seem to be saying that people should be encouraged to do
something they would otherwise not be able to do, when in fact a great
many of them seem well equipped to do so and to do so with ease. French
philosopher Michel Foucault described a similar irony. He pointed out that
those who write about sexuality—such as sex educators or sexologists—
often claim they are trying to open up sexuality for public discussion and
overcome public resistance to such discussion and reticence to think about
or discuss sex. Yet, of course, they make such arguments in a modern world
that is dripping with sexuality, in which everybody seems preoccupied with
sex and in which talk about sex is almost impossible to escape.[30] Likewise,
in a world of self-preoccupied individualists, advocates of self-esteem feel it
is necessary to reassure people that attention to the self is socially and
morally acceptable and desirable.

MOTIVES AND MOTIVATIONS

A second general route to understanding how the ideas and practices of
teachers, with respect to self-esteem, realize a culture of individualism is
through their influence on motivation and vocabularies of motive.[31] The
general principle is that ideas about motivation—which every culture
has—provide people with motives and, in fact, structure both their psyches
and social activities in ways that are at least partially consistent with these
ideas. Again, to grasp this important point, we must suspend belief in the
idea that self-esteem is a fundamental motive or that human beings naturally seek approval and acceptance, and we must instead examine these as
culturally imbedded ideas.

Every culture not only maintains a set of beliefs about what causes or
motivates human beings to act as they do but provides a vocabulary (and
sometimes several different vocabularies) that people can use to talk about
their behavior. In the world of contemporary American business, for example, people believe in the "profit motive." That is, they believe people are
fundamentally self-interested, that they naturally and legitimately seek to
do things that will benefit themselves. Such beliefs shape individuals' perceptions of the world, so they are on the lookout for profitable business
opportunities. At the same time, these beliefs serve to justify behavior, to
make it right in the eyes of the business person and others. A store owner
who drives a competitor out of business by undercutting prices thinks of

such an activity not only as proper but as an expression of the natural order of things, and would likely argue that it would be foolish to do otherwise. "After all," the owner might say, "if I don't compete, my competitor will drive me out of business!"

Many cultures—perhaps especially those in the modern world—contain several sets of beliefs about motivation, each one operating within a specific sphere of activity and thought to explain and justify actions taken within it. The individual who thinks in terms of profit, competition, and victory when acting as a businessperson, probably would think it was outrageous to apply the same assumptions when he or she returned home from the shop. Spouses do not ordinarily regard one another as competitors, or evaluate possible actions toward one another in terms of potential profit or loss. Rather, they think of "love" and "commitment" and "self-sacrifice" as the causes of and justification for their actions. In this sphere, people think it is natural not to seek profit in everything they do, but rather to fulfill obligations to people they love, to do without material things they want or need so a child can have an education, or to give emotional support without any thought of gain. What seems eminently reasonable in the world of business is almost unthinkable within the family.

The existence of different ideas about the causes of and reasons for behavior within different spheres of activity leads to some difficult questions. What really motivates people to act? Are human beings fundamentally self-interested? Are they also driven by considerations of love and obligation? Do they naturally and inevitably seek to enhance self-esteem? Are some motives more important than others?

These questions are inherently unanswerable as stated, because they assume there is something basic and universal about human motives that can be grasped, apart from a particular culture and its ideas about motivation. There are several reasons to be wary of this assumption and of the approach to human motivation on which it is based. First, we can observe what people *say* about their behavior, but the underlying drives, needs, or inclinations we attribute to them are hidden from us. We observe the "profit motive" or "self-sacrifice" in what people say about their conduct, or in what others say about them, but we cannot directly see the underlying psychic conditions that prompt the cutthroat businesswoman or adoring father to behave as they do. Indeed, such underlying psychic conditions probably are as hidden from the individual as they are from the external observer. Sometimes we do not know why we act as we do—we find ourselves developing a competitive attitude toward a friend and acting in competitive ways, but we become conscious of doing so only after the fact. We may search for reasons for our conduct, but the "motives" or "reasons" we attribute may or may not capture what really spurred us to act as we did.

Second, because human beings are cultural creatures, dependent on complex cultural learning rather than raw biology or simple conditioning, there may well be no inherent or universal human motives. To be sure, we can find evidence of such fundamental drives as sex, hunger, or survival, but these are so general as to be almost useless in explaining behavior. Human beings express their sexual or food "drives" in a great variety of ways. Moreover, however powerful the "will to live" might be, human beings seem uniquely capable of putting it aside, as, for example, when they commit suicide or sacrifice their own lives for those of others. Like the instincts enumerated by social scientists at the beginning of the twentieth century, so-called universal motives such as "self-esteem" or "self-interest" seem capable of explaining everything, for it is easy to invent motives (as it was instincts) to explain a particular kind of behavior one wants to explain. But what explains everything really explains nothing.

Finally, whenever we observe human beings, we observe them as participants who have, in a particular culture, absorbed its assumptions and speak about themselves in the vocabulary it provides. There really is no such thing as a human being who is free of such cultural influence, whose motivation can be observed or inspected. Rather, there are people who have been shaped by their culture, who view themselves and their world as they have learned to view it, and who conceive of themselves and their actions in terms their culture provides.

It seems more useful then to think of human motives as supplied by culture and of human beings as being motivated by the forces their culture establishes as significant. If a particular culture teaches that human beings are self-interested and provides a vocabulary for describing and justifying the pursuit of self-interest, then people will be motivated by self-interest. If the culture teaches that human beings are fundamentally oriented toward securing the approval of others and thus enhancing their self-esteem, and if it provides them with a rich language for expressing these ideas, then participants in this culture will be motivated by the quest for approval and self-esteem. Indeed, those—such as psychologists—who study such people will "discover" that self-interest, approval, or self-esteem are fundamental human needs and motives. This is not surprising, of course, because they are studying people whom the culture has constructed in this manner.

Seen in this light, teachers who promote the importance of self-esteem in the classroom are engaged in creating the forms of motivation thought to be natural in their culture. That is, by acting toward their students as if they naturally craved approval, recognition, attention, or self-esteem, they are in fact helping to create people who crave these things. They do so because they provide not only the terms through which they grasp or explain the behavior of their students, but also because they provide the terms students are likely to use themselves. Students come to think that they need attention or seek self-esteem, and they do so because they use the words that have been provided to them as a way of understanding themselves. Self-esteem becomes important because it is thought to be important, and it comes to motivate behavior because we say that it does.

This approach to motivation requires two qualifications. First, culture tends to provide multiple vocabularies of motive rather than a single vocabulary. Because each set of assumptions about motivation tends to operate within a particular sphere of activity, we cannot assume that a vocabulary that shapes motivation within a particular context will do so in some other context. Teachers who emphasize self-esteem and put their students through some of the exercises described earlier may well be shaping people who are motivated by a need for approval, recognition, or self-esteem. But these same pupils are exposed to other vocabularies in other situations, and they are likely to think and act within those contexts in ways they have learned are acceptable. The child who learns to think in terms of recognition or acceptance in the classroom may face an entirely different set of expectations at home, where parents may emphasize the fulfillment of obligations or subservience to authority as basic ways of thinking and talking about conduct.

The second qualification is more complex, and I will explore it in greater detail in Chapter 5. Briefly, I believe American culture provides its participants with vocabularies of motive that often conflict with one another, even within particular situations or social contexts. Up to this point, I have argued that people learn to adopt a set of ideas about behavior and motivation and apply them within particular situations—economic motives in business contexts, motives of commitment and self-sacrifice in the family, religious motives in church or synagogue. But cultures also tend to make life difficult for people by providing them with alternative motives, even within the same social situation. Many teachers and students in schools, for example, believe that people have an unqualified right to acceptance and respect. But others hold an opposite set of beliefs, namely that acceptance and respect, and the self-esteem they provide, should be earned, that they are not things to which all are entitled but rather things that some deserve because they have earned the right to them. As I will show later, there is considerable conflict over the educational theory of self-esteem, which has opponents who are every bit as vocal as its advocates. Thus, we cannot assume teachers who espouse the theory are fully successful in creating people motivated by self-esteem, since they and their students encounter opposing views of human nature.

In general terms, then, the educational theory of self-esteem provides teachers and students with a vocabulary of motives that realizes at least some of the culture's assumptions about individuals and their rights and capabilities. It does so by creating people who, at least part of the time or in certain social situations, are motivated precisely as the theory says. But they are so motivated not because that is the natural human order of things but because culture constructs them to be so motivated.

HOPE AND THE ILLUSION OF ACTION

The self-esteem theory of education is rooted in a culture that exalts the individual and puts the self on center stage, but it is more than individualism that makes this theory appealing and accounts for its widespread adoption. When ideas become as popular as the belief in the power of self-esteem has, it is likely to be so not only because the idea has deep cultural roots and is successfully promoted by conceptual entrepreneurs but also because it is useful. Thus, we must ask, why is self-esteem such a useful idea in education? The answer, I will argue, is that self-esteem is a solution in search of problems, and that in the field of education it has met spectacular success in finding one.[32]

A solution in search of a problem? This seems to be an odd way of putting the matter. Ordinarily, we think, human beings encounter problems of various kinds, and when they do they seek solutions to those problems. A married couple, for example, begin quarreling and at some point recognize this as a problem, attempt to figure out why they are always at one another's throats, and then take action to solve the problem. A company discovers it is losing its market share, studies the problem and decides its products are perceived as being too expensive for their features or quality, thus takes steps to improve the quality (or perception of the quality) or reduce the price. First there is a problem, then a diagnosis of the problem, and finally a solution, based on the diagnosis.

No doubt things sometimes work this way in both interpersonal and organizational life, but often they seem to work in almost the opposite way. People perceive a problem they feel must be solved. But instead of looking for a solution based on a careful diagnosis of the problem, they invoke a solution that readily comes to mind and to which they may already be committed, and they then begin to perceive the problem through the lens provided by the solution. A quarrelling married couple, for example, who decide they have had enough verbal battles, may come up with the idea that they need to "improve communication." "We wouldn't fight so much if we communicated more effectively," they may agree; "Our problem is really a problem of communication." In this illustration, a solution—better communication—comes to be the framework in terms of which the couple perceive the reality of their situation. They begin to talk about past misunderstandings, about the difficulties they have had expressing feelings to one another, about instances where quarrels have been precipitated by "lack of communication." They ignore quarrels where perhaps there was no failure of communication—where it may have been precisely the clear understanding of their differences that led to the conflict. They invoke whatever generalizations they can command to buttress their points of view. And they seek concrete lines of activity that will improve communication. As they do so, the problem becomes constructed in such a way that the solution fits; the ready-made cure turns out to be just what the doctor ordered, and hopefully they look forward to renewed marital harmony.

A popular aphorism expresses this idea in simpler terms: to a person with a hammer, every problem looks like a nail. Likewise, to teachers and teacher educators armed with a theory of self-esteem, every educational problem looks like a problem of low self-esteem. The theory of self-esteem is ready-made: it has been created by social scientists and marketed by conceptual entrepreneurs. It fits a culture in which the individual is important and the self is central. And, most important, it seems to make sense of the vexing problems of academic failure, lack of motivation, and student rebellion. Self-esteem becomes just what the educational doctor ordered. Problems of educational failure become perceived as problems of self-esteem, and courses of action are developed that will improve self-esteem. The authority of psychologists is sought, and educators tailor their theories to meet the needs of the classroom. More and more, problem and solution seem to go hand in glove, and teachers take heart from the conviction that there is something they can do to deal with the problems of education.

Such ready-made solutions—which I will henceforth call *quasi-theories*—have two fundamental characteristics that help explain why they are so enthusiastically adopted, used, and defended. First, quasi-theories direct action, providing specific lines of conduct for people to follow and a rationale for these actions. Second, quasi-theories introduce a sense of hope into situations that would otherwise seem hopeless, for they provide people with a sense that they are doing things that will eventually solve their problems. The quasi-theory of self-esteem tells teachers, parents, and even students what to do, explains why they should do it, and provides them with a reason for being optimistic that things will improve in the future.

In the United States, education has become defined in the last few decades as one of our most serious and vexing problems. Achievement test scores have declined, student mastery of subject matter has weakened, and behavioral problems in the schools have multiplied. Although the problems are often regarded as most acute for minority students, they are perceived as affecting students in almost all school systems in the country. The educational system is widely believed to be in decline, beset with violence, and no longer capable of producing graduates with the skills needed to sustain an advanced economy. Whether the problems of education are greater or lesser than the perception of them is, of course, a different issue. The crucial point is that there is a widely perceived problem.

A variety of solutions have been thrown at the problems of education: Increased discipline. Higher academic standards. Higher pay for teachers. Police officers in the schools. School choice. Magnet schools. A return to the basics of education—the three Rs. In other words, a variety of quasi-theories have been invoked to define and solve the problems of education. Each solution constructs the problem in a way that renders it susceptible to action. Each posits specific lines of conduct that will, it is hoped, eventually lead to better educational systems.

The quasi-theory of self-esteem provides specific things that teachers can do to help their students and thus solve the problems, or some of the problems, of education. It makes it possible for teachers—at least those who subscribe to the theory—to enter the classroom, confident that they have something to give their students that will improve their lives. As children perform the various exercises, the teacher can see the looks of happiness or accomplishment on their faces as they receive praise or recognition. At the end of each day, the teacher can look back with a sense of accomplishment, knowing he or she has done something that is likely to have long-lasting effects. And at the beginning of each day—and each new school year—the teacher has grounds for feeling hopeful that something will be accomplished, that children who might otherwise be lost will be saved, that failure can turn into triumph.

If there were clear evidence that improving self-esteem has the impact that its proponents claim for it—and there is not—then we could account for the persistence of the theory on the grounds that people stick with it because it works. But the evidence that would support this theory does not exist. Plenty of data show that students who achieve higher grades have higher self-esteem, but such correlational data do not establish that improving self-esteem leads to improved achievement. The associations that exist are weak, not strong. And there are no long-term studies that show the efficacy of widely used methods for enhancing self-esteem.[33]

If self-esteem is not really the powerful solution educators believe it is, how can we account for the widespread faith in it and the belief that it works? There are at least three reasons why the theory persists, in spite of the scarcity of supporting evidence. First, the very activities of enhancing self-esteem are satisfying and rewarding to many teachers, for clearly making another human being feel good about himself or herself also makes one feel good about oneself. The everyday classroom situation tends to focus attention on both the teacher's and students' time and energy put into the activity—on the inputs, which are themselves rewarding, rather than the long-term outputs. Second, no one claims children improve over night, for severe damage has been done to many of them and healing takes time. For some, it is felt the road to a better self-image and academic success is a long one, and it may take years of effort before results are seen. However, the yearly parade of children through the classroom and on to the next grade provides a constantly refreshed and changing set of selves to enhance, selves that fade from scrutiny and memory each year as a new set arrives. The teacher must take his or her students' eventual improvement on faith, for he or she will likely not see most of them again. And third, the means chosen to pursue an end sometimes becomes an end in itself. Self-esteem is advanced as a key to improving students' educational life chances, but it is not difficult for the improvement of self-regard to become a major goal in itself. As the objectives and assigned responsibilities of educators have expanded generally over the past half-century, it is not surprising to find that the "education of the self" (as one teacher-educator termed his subject matter) has become defined as important in itself.[34]

Self-esteem is an appealing and persisting theory also because it fits well with what seems to be an increased emphasis on feelings in the culture as a whole. Educators have expanded their sense of responsibility and claims of expertise to encompass the child's emotional well-being in a culture that has itself begun to pay more attention to emotional well-being. Professional psychotherapy is widely utilized by the middle classes as well as by those whose health insurance policies cover mental illness. Various popular and alternative therapeutic methods have flourished in the last three decades, aided by the New Age movement and by a generalized interest in alternative health systems. Successful treatments for mood disorders such as depression and anxiety have begun to establish the idea that healthy people have the right to feel good and feel good about themselves. It is not surprising then that the myth of self-esteem can survive even without convincing empirical evidence of its truth.

Thus the theory of self-esteem persists because it is useful and believable. It is useful because it makes teachers and their students hopeful about the future and provides for the illusion, if not the reality, of constructive action. It is believable because it fits with broader cultural currents and ideas and, in fact, helps realize them.

AVOIDING INEQUALITY

One additional line of analysis illuminates the myth of self-esteem and helps account for its success, and that involves the connection between self-esteem and inequality. Much of the discussion of self-esteem in schools focuses directly or implicitly on inequalities among students. It is argued, for example, that children make judgments of one another based on physical appearance or prowess, thus damaging the self-esteem of children judged fat or ugly or uncoordinated. In this instance, damaged self-esteem is held to create inequalities among students, since those with damaged

self-esteem will not do as well in school. Moreover, the very existence of damaged self-esteem is a form of inequality, since all are entitled to have a good
self-image. Educators also pay a great deal of attention to the ways in which
class, race, and gender influence self-esteem. It is argued that the self-esteem
of poor and minority children, for example, suffers because of their social
backgrounds, and that schools engage in practices that lower the self-esteem
of adolescent girls. Here, existing inequalities lead to lowered self-esteem,
which implies as well that even greater inequalities are likely to develop.

This emphasis on inequality as a threat to self-esteem, and low self-
esteem as something that perpetuates inequality, on the surface seems to be
a socially conscious and progressive development within education. Those
children society oppresses because of their race, ethnicity, social class, or
gender, the argument runs, are denied something—self-esteem—which is
essential if they are to overcome their oppression. Because they come to
think of themselves as society thinks of them, children feel less worthy, less
good, and less capable. With their motivation and self-confidence thus
reduced, these children come to accept the place society has assigned to
them. They aspire to low-paying jobs that require less education and skill.
They learn not to challenge the existing social order; indeed, they see themselves as the powerful members of the society wish them to see themselves.

Several problems lurk below the surface of this line of thinking. First,
research evidence does not unequivocally support the claim that minori-
ties, women, or the poor suffer the kinds of damage to self-esteem that the
myth of self-esteem asserts.[35] Moreover, in the more than half-century since
the end of World War II, a variety of social groups in the United States have
strenuously resisted social inequality and endeavored to keep racism, sexism, and social class on the national agenda. The picture one has of African
Americans, women, or working-class people is not one of psychically
wounded people unable to fend for themselves or lacking the motivation to
learn or work. Rather, one sees people actively resisting oppression in ways
available to them, charged with energy that derives from a collective sense
of identity and social worth.

There is irony, then, in the discussion of the oppression of racism, sexism, or classism in terms of lowered self-esteem and wounded psyches.
Those who define their own oppression partly in terms of its effect on self-
esteem seem to belie their own claims, through their own vigorous protest
and expression of pride in race, gender, and class. They often seem to be too
energetic and proud to suffer from the low self-esteem they claim as theirs.
Those who make claims of psychic oppression on behalf of the oppressed
seem largely unaware of this irony and of the research evidence. The suspi-
cion arises then that for both the oppressed and their advocates the language of self-esteem functions in ways unrelated to the substantive claims
of the myth of self-esteem.

Although the myth of self-esteem implicitly and explicitly criticizes social inequalities of various kinds, it is a blunted and misleading critique in the hands of those who advocate for the oppressed. It is so largely because, very much in the general spirit of American culture, it individualizes the discussion of inequality, portraying it largely in terms of its effects on the individual and seeking solutions that are by and large individual solutions. The discourse of self-esteem tends, to use C. Wright Mills' terms, to make inequality a "personal trouble" rather than a "public issue."[36] It is the individual person inequality damages, in the eyes of teachers who decry racism or sexism and seek to reverse its effects in the classroom. And it is the individual who must change in order to overcome these effects.

Conceiving of social inequality largely in terms of its effects on individuals has a major problem and a significant consequence. The major problem is that this individualized conception of inequality proposes solutions to the problems of racism or sexism that by themselves cannot conceivably overcome these social forces. Even highly motivated and self-liking people whose self-esteem has been improved in school and who have been academically successful will face some barriers to success on the basis of race or gender. Unless individuals have access to education, training, jobs, and housing, their motivation and competence will not take them very far. These good things must exist for people to have access to them—there must be available jobs, for example, for those who are motivated to do them. Although it is hard to deny that poverty, racism, or sexism are demoralizing and tend to sap energy and initiative, restoring energy and initiative alone does not remove the socially structured inequalities of access to education and jobs.

The significant consequence of this individualized and indirect discourse about inequality through the myth of self-esteem is to distract attention from inequality itself. Numerous observers have pointed to the fact that Americans discuss social class only with great difficulty. Ours is a society in which an economically diverse majority of people think of themselves as "middle class," and are apt to oppose such measures as progressive income taxes even when they earn low enough incomes to benefit from them. The myth of self-esteem further distracts attention from social inequality, because it focuses attention on individual effort and initiative rather than on the social order. By doing so, it competes, in effect, with alternative explanations. To some extent, a chorus of voices in praise of self-esteem merely drowns out the voices of others who argue that it is the social system itself that produces and perpetuates inequality. In a culture already focused on the individual and convinced of the powers individuals can bring to bear to lift themselves, the myth of self-esteem also serves as "evidence" of this belief.

What about those who claim injury to self-esteem as a part of their more general oppression or victimization? What can account for the wide-spread adoption of the myth of self-esteem by those whose own vigorous resistance signifies healthy self-esteem? If the myth of self-esteem individu-alizes inequality, it arguably works against the interests of the victims of inequality. Why then do they support the myth?

The answer may lie partly in the current ascendancy of feelings and emotional well-being in the culture as a whole. The myth of self-esteem draws into its orbit even those who might otherwise be suspicious of it, because discourse about emotions exerts a profound cultural gravity on the thoughts and words of everyone. The plethora of articles, books, talk show discussions, sermons, and other forms of talk about self-esteem makes all highly conscious of self-esteem, impediments to self-esteem, means of improving self-esteem, and beneficial consequences of high self-esteem. Voices speaking of self-esteem effectively drown out voices offering other explanations—or at the very least make it more difficult for other such voices to be heard.

Self-interest may also, somewhat paradoxically, account for the use of the language of self-esteem by victimized groups. The very currency of the language affords an opportunity to describe victimization in terms that may elicit sympathy. Even if the factual basis of claims for self-esteem is quite shaky, the language of self-esteem at least provides a common ground between victim and potential sympathetic allies. The risk of using the lan-guage of psychic wounding, of course, is that others will see one as unable to fend for oneself. The potential gain is at least they will see one as victim-ized and in need of better, fairer, and more equitable and less damaging treatment. Moreover, the concept of self-esteem is so flexible that it can eas-ily stretch to legitimate efforts to ground self-esteem in group identifica-tion. From the standpoint of victimized groups, at present the remedy for social injustice and wounded self-esteem is group affiliation, in which cause they ironically enlist the individualistic language of self-esteem.

STRETCHING MEANINGS

The flexible meaning of self-esteem is, in fact, among the most interesting social facts about this concept. The myth of self-esteem seems ready to travel from one ideological world to another, to be put to whatever uses its sellers and buyers wish. There seem to be few if any uses to which it cannot be put. This elastic meaning poses a problem for our understanding of this phenomenon. How can one word take on so many apparent meanings? Why does it do so? My next task is to examine the nature of and reasons for this flexibility and to address such questions.

NOTES

1. Jack Canfield and Harold Wells, *100 Ways to Enhance Self-Concept in the Classroom: A Handbook for Teachers and Parents.* Englewood Cliffs, N.J.: Prentice-Hall, 1976.
2. Bettie B. Youngs, *The Six Vital Ingredients of Self-Esteem: How to Develop Them in Your Students.* Rolling Hills Estates, Calif.: Jalmar Press, 1992, 3–5.
3. James Dobson, "The Greatest Gift You Can Give to Your Child." *Reader's Digest* 127, December 1985: 126.
4. Karen Owens, *Raising Your Child's Inner Self-Esteem.* New York: Plenum, 1995.
5. Anne C. Bernstein, "Feeling Great (About Myself): How Can You Help Your Child Feel Self-Confident and Resilient?" *Parents' Magazine* 57, September 1982: 51.
6. Selma Wassermann, "Enabling Children to Develop Personal Power Through Building Self-Respect." *Childhood Education* 63, April 1987: 294.
7. Ibid.
8. Myrna J. Folkins, "Can Do: Tips for Helping Your Child." *Parents' Magazine* 63, May 1988: 70.
9. Patricia H. Berne, "Seven Secrets for Building Kids Self-Esteem." *Instructor* 94, November–December 1985: 29.
10. Youngs, op. cit.
11. Randy M. Page and Tana S. Page, *Fostering Emotional Well-Being in the Classroom.* Boston: Jones and Bartlett, 1993.
12. Dobson, ibid.
13. Ibid., 127.
14. Canfield and Wells, op. cit.
15. Shayle Uroff, "Apollo High School: Achievement through Self-Esteem." *Educational Leadership* 46, February 1989: 80.
16. Mary Harbaugh, "The Power of Self-Esteem: Can a Second-Grade Teacher Prepare Kids to Refuse Drugs Several Years Down the Road? Just Ask Juanita Pierce." *Instructor* 99, January 1990: 45.
17. Rose M. Higdon, "Pride . . . a Continuing Classroom Campaign." *Instructor* 95, February 1986: 36.
18. Ibid.
19. Valerie W. Wesley, "Taking Back Our Schools." *Essence* magazine 20, February 1990: 102.
20. Rosemary L. Bray, "Self-Esteem: Hoax or Reality?" The *New York Times* 140, November 4, 1990: 4A.
21. Canfield and Wells, op. cit., 182. Emphasis in original.

22. Canfield and Wells, op. cit., 78.
23. Debbie McNamara, "How to Teach Pride." *Instructor* 95, February 1986: 34.
24. Berne, op. cit., 62.
25. Youngs, op. cit., 97.
26. Uroff, op. cit., 80.
27. Wassermann, op. cit., 294. Emphasis added.
28. Youngs, op. cit., 70.
29. See especially Christopher Lasch, *The Culture of Narcissism* (New York: Basic Books, 1978); and Robert N. Bellah, Richard Madsen, William M. Sullivan, Ann Swidler, and Steven M. Tipton, *Habits of the Heart: Individualism and Commitment in American Life* (Berkeley: University of California Press, 1985).
30. Michel Foucault, *History of Sexuality*, Vol. I.
31. This discussion draws upon John P. Hewitt, *Self and Society: A Symbolic Interactionist Social Psychology,* 7th ed., 31 (Boston: Allyn and Bacon, 1997); and C. Wright Mills, "Situated Actions and Vocabularies of Motive." *American Sociological Review* 5 (October 1940: 905–913).
32. This view of the relationship between problems and solutions is developed in Peter M. Hall and John P. Hewitt, "The Quasi-theory of Communication and the Management of Dissent." *Social Problems* 18 (Summer 1970: 17–27); and in John P. Hewitt and Peter M. Hall, "Social Problems, Problematic Situations, and Quasi-theories." *American Sociological Review* 38 (June 1973: 67–74).
33. For a review of this literature, see Martin V. Covington, "Self-Esteem and Failure in School: Analysis and Policy Implications" in *The Social Importance of Self-Esteem,* eds. Andrew M. Mecca, Neil J. Smelser, and John Vasconcellos. (Berkeley, Calif.: University of California Press, 1989), 72–124.
34. Gerald Weinstein, Joy Hardin, and Matt Weinstein, *Education of the Self: A Trainer's Manual.* New York: Irvington, 1982.
35. See Morris Rosenberg and Leonard I. Perlin, "Social Class and Self-Esteem Among Children and Adults." *American Journal of Sociology* 84, 1978: 54–77; and Morris Rosenberg and Roberta G. Simmons, *Black and White Self-Esteem: The Urban School Child.* Washington, D. C.: The American Sociological Association, 1972.
36. C. Wright Mills, *The Sociological Imagination.* New York: Oxford University Press, 1959.

5

A Word for All Seasons

The ideas about self-esteem and the uses of the concept that we have examined point to a key fact about this word: Self-esteem can mean almost anything the therapist, commentator, preacher, teacher, critic, or casual user wants it to mean. Self-esteem also precipitates controversy, for some people reject the word and the ideas it represents just as fervently as others endorse them. It is a word for all seasons.

The varied meanings of self-esteem and the disagreements it engenders are the major focus of this chapter. How can a word so commonly used have so many meanings? How can a word that seems well-suited to express basic American ideas about the self arouse heated disagreement? I will begin to answer these questions by summarizing the key meanings of self-esteem that we have encountered thus far. Then I will attempt to explain this diversity of meaning by showing how American culture creates such divergent points of view. Finally, I will turn to the controversies about self-esteem as an additional source of insight into its cultural significance.

ONE WORD, MANY MEANINGS

To grasp the varied and often contradictory meanings of self-esteem we must examine the dimensions along which use of the word varies. There are at least four such dimensions: the sources of self-esteem, the rationale for acquiring it, the demands acquiring or maintaining it make upon the individual, and the very nature of self-esteem. Each of these dimensions of meaning consists of divergent or opposite ideas about self-esteem; each is an axis along which the meaning of self-esteem varies. These dimensions shape the way we think about self-esteem. They provide the key alternatives we consider when we use the term, especially when controversies arise about where it comes from, why it is important, what people must do to get it, and its very essence. They structure our thinking about self-esteem in ways that resemble Americans' more general ideas about themselves and their society.

The first dimension focuses on the ultimate *source* of self-esteem, specifically whether it lies within the power of the individual or derives from the social world. People often think of self-esteem as a state of mind or feeling that in the last analysis depends on the individual and lies within his or her own control. Those who argue, for example, that only people who accept themselves for what they are will develop self-esteem rely on the assumption that self-esteem is ultimately the individual's responsibility. Those who claim self-esteem can only be earned through achievement in some form, such as working for good grades in school or making a success of oneself in a career, take the same position. So do those who believe the individual can attain self-esteem through some form of psychic bootstrapping, such as the various forms of self-talk. These various beliefs about the nature of self-esteem differ markedly in other respects, of course. Those who believe self-esteem must be earned through achievement would scorn those who think the key lies merely in self-acceptance. But they share the conviction that individuals hold the power to shape their own self-esteem.

The contrasting position holds that self-esteem derives from the social world and that it is not exclusively or even mainly under the individual's control. Teachers who believe that one of their chief duties is to support and enhance their students' self-esteem take this position, as do parents who believe they are ultimately responsible for raising children with good self-esteem. So do social scientists, who emphasize that attitudes toward the self reflect both the social world's treatment of the individual and the person's interpretations of that treatment. And Afro-centrists who argue that the self-esteem of African-American children must be grounded in knowledge of their culture and identification with it also invoke this belief. The proponents of these various ideas might disagree sharply with one another in other ways, but they share the view that self-esteem has its origins in the social world.

This axis of meaning is only occasionally made explicit when people talk or write about self-esteem. Like other dimensions along which everyday meanings vary, it rises to the surface of consciousness when challenged in some way. A teacher who urges children to repeat the phrase "I am lovable and capable" in a school classroom, for example, acts on the assumption that the teacher and students share responsibility for the students' self-esteem. For teachers, this is a matter of fact, a secure part of what they know about the world and not something that needs discussing. Only if someone, such as a parent or school principal, objects that the exercise is a waste of valuable time that could more productively be devoted to learning math or spelling are assumptions about the origins of self-esteem likely to be made explicit. In that situation, the teacher will seek some way of justifying the exercise, and thus begin to discuss the sources of self-esteem.

As this illustration suggests, it is possible to speak and act in ways that support opposing principles or ideas about self-esteem. The teacher (by leading the exercise) is acting on the secure belief that he or she must try to enhance a child's self-esteem, but also on the belief that self-esteem lies within a child's own control (repeating an idea, it is held, reinforces it). Some proponents of one or another method for improving self-esteem argue that these positions are mutually exclusive—that self-esteem derives either from the individual or society. Others argue that both are valid assumptions, that the polarity is false. Some generally emphasize one position without questioning its opposite.

Such dimensions of meaning reveal something about the way people in a particular social world think—the alternative explanations they consider, the options they believe open to them, the choices they think possible or necessary. When people invoke propositions about the individual or social nature of self-esteem, they are revealing how they think about the individual's relationship to society. To say that "self-esteem lies within each person's grasp" or that "we owe it to our children to give them the best self-esteem we can" is to specify how one views that relationship. This axis of meaning indicates that Americans distinguish sharply between the person and the society, and that the relationship between the two is something they worry about, something that can be a matter of deep disagreement or argument.

A second dimension of meaning focuses on whether self-esteem is mainly to be thought of as a desirable end or chiefly as a means to other ends. Much of what is said about self-esteem seems to rest on the view that high self-esteem is in itself an inherently desirable goal. Those who argue that self-esteem is something to which everyone is entitled, or that it is a basic measure of the individual's health, as important to mental health as a healthy heart is to the body, take this position. So do those who assert that self-esteem is a fundamental human motivation, that it drives human conduct as surely as a quest for food or sexual fulfillment. Whether the source of self-esteem is thought to be the individual, the social world, or both, the important issue at stake is why it is important. And the answer often given is that self-esteem is important in its own right, as a significant and even necessary measure of the quality of human experience.

The opposing view of self-esteem takes a far more utilitarian position, arguing that self-esteem is important not in itself but rather for what it accomplishes for the individual or society as a whole. Educationists who claim that self-esteem can be taught to children and that it is a prerequisite to their achievement in school take this instrumental view of self-esteem. So do those who argue that improving self-esteem will help solve the problems of out-of-wedlock pregnancy, child abuse, or delinquency. And business consultants who tell corporations that improving their workers' self-esteem will help the bottom line also express this point of view.

Like the previous axis, this one reveals something about the underlying basis on which people think about themselves and their actions. The assumptions they make about the social world can be thought of as ways of rendering their actions legitimate. Human beings need to have the sense that their actions are appropriate or legitimate, and one way of creating that feeling is by appealing to what they consider to be factual knowledge. Legitimacy can be thought of as a place where the mind comes to rest, where no further questions about the rightness of conduct need to be asked or answered. Urging readers that everybody has the right to a positive self-image is thus an effort to lend legitimacy to actions one is recommending by treating this right as a matter of fact.

A third axis of meaning centers on beliefs about whether individuals change or remain the same when their self-esteem improves. Enhanced or improved self-esteem often is associated with efforts to change the individual. Improved self-esteem may be seen as a necessary prerequisite to changing the person for the better, or perhaps as the beneficial consequence of other changes that are desirable in their own right. In either case, there is a strong assumption that improving self-esteem and changing the person go hand-in-hand. The argument that improved self-esteem enhances learning or occupational success makes this assumption, as does the belief that those who eliminate negative feelings about themselves will be happier.

Some assertions about self-esteem invoke the opposite position, arguing that enhanced self-esteem should not depend on or even precipitate any more far-reaching changes in the person. The assertion that self-esteem requires only unconditional self-acceptance adopts this perspective, for it explicitly argues that the individual need not change anything about himself or herself to gain self-esteem—the person need not lose weight, do better in school, or earn more money to acquire self-esteem. Likewise, the argument that children should be given unconditional love by parents and teachers takes the same position.

Again, this axis of meaning reveals something about how Americans think about the person. Regardless of whether a particular view of self-esteem sees personal change as necessary, inevitable, irrelevant, or undesirable, their understanding of self-esteem depends upon its association with change. When they argue that people deserve self-esteem regardless of what they do, they are implicitly anchoring their views in relation to this more general assumption about change. Just as they might seek legitimacy for their views in the assumption that self-esteem is a valuable end in its own right, they seek legitimacy in their assumptions about individuals and their right to remain the same.

The fourth dimension of meaning involves the very nature of self-esteem. Much of the contemporary discourse about self-esteem is based on the conviction that *feelings* are not only a crucial aspect of human experi-

---

ence in general but also lie at the heart of self-esteem. But the kinds of feelings associated with self-esteem differ. One view asserts that self-esteem rests essentially upon the person's capacity to *feel good* about himself or herself. Those who argue that self-esteem depends on self-acceptance or self-liking most clearly base their views on this position. So do those whose programs for improving self-esteem entail the repetition of positive statements about the self, particularly in a group setting. A classroom filled with students cheering themselves on with animated repetitions of phrases such as "I am somebody," for example, seems designed not merely to alter students' cognition of themselves but more crucially to create a mood in which self-feeling is enhanced. From this perspective, self-esteem seems associated with "good moods" and "feeling good about oneself" and "happiness."

In contrast, self-esteem also carries the meaning of *self-respect*, which emphasizes a different form of affect. "Feeling good about oneself" conveys a relatively undifferentiated positive mood that is aroused by reflecting on oneself or interacting with approving others. "Self-respect" has a different set of connotations, for it is likely to be associated with specific actions or personal attributes that often are associated with the word "character." Just as the root word "respect" has the connotative meaning of "deference" and "honor" toward another person, so self-respect carries the same meaning with respect to the self. Those who assume self-esteem is grounded in—or equivalent to—self-respect are implicitly thinking of deference, honor, appreciation, character, and specific accomplishment when they use the term.

Those who urge drug abusers to recover their self-esteem by abstaining from the use of drugs provide a good illustration of the assumption that self-esteem means self-respect. Their usage ties self-esteem to a specific action, namely overcoming the temptation to abuse drugs. Abstinence—which may require the help of others but which in the last analysis is the individual's responsibility—becomes a mark of character, therefore an indication that the person has earned the respect not only of others but of himself or herself.

CULTURE AND DISCOURSE

The dimensions along which the meaning of self-esteem varies when people speak of it in classrooms, on TV talk shows, in magazine articles, or in personal conversations pose a significant problem for our understanding of the myth of self-esteem. How can a word that is so widely used have so many potential and frequently opposite meanings? Why do these diverse and contradictory meanings exist?

Although there are many possible answers to these questions, I will offer a cultural interpretation. Words like self-esteem are symptomatic of the culture in which they are used. They tell us something about the way those who share that culture see the world, about what they take for granted about it. Such words tell us something about culture in its classic meaning of the "ways of thinking, feeling, and acting shared by the members of a community." When such words have contradictory meanings, they indicate the presence of cultural disagreements. When words elicit divergent responses, they are evidence of polarization and of serious fissures in the culture.

"Cultural disagreements," "polarization," and "fissures" are very abstract terms, and to show their relationship to self-esteem I must provide a bit of theoretical background to make them more concrete. I begin by considering the nature of culture.

Generally, social scientists view culture as the established ways of thinking, feeling, and acting of a particular society. Culture thus encompasses language, ideas, empirical knowledge, norms and values, and a myriad of behavioral recipes that guide people in their everyday lives. Culture defines the foods they prefer to eat and those they find repulsive. It is the source of their ideas about God or gods, it urges them to value friendship or honesty or self-interest, and it shows them how to plant corn, change the oil in a car engine, and perform open-heart surgery. Culture seems to be a set of organized solutions to the problems that confront human beings, a set of answers to their anxious questions about the nature of their world, and a source of reassuring knowledge and belief.

Although this is a helpful way of looking at culture, it is not the whole story.[1] In some ways, culture is a source of problems as well as solutions: it gives rise to many of the anxious questions it seeks to answer, and it makes people worry about what they can or should do rather than reassuring them about what they are doing. Elsewhere I have argued that American culture creates a characteristic set of dilemmas that many people experience and must find ways to resolve.[2] It encourages people to put down roots in a community, yet it also promotes an urge to pull them up and seek greener pastures elsewhere. It makes conformity simultaneously a virtue and a vice and rebellion is something to be both sought and avoided. At the same time, as it puts the individual on center stage, it celebrates the value of community and the need for intimacy.

We can see these dilemmas in a variety of concrete circumstances. Parents want their growing children to declare their independence and strike out on their own, yet often find it difficult to let go of them or accept their decisions to strike out in new directions. Parents want their children to obey the rules, especially their rules, yet they often take pride in their children's rebelliousness. Adolescents seem to resist the urge to do and be what their parents want, yet they readily conform to the dictates of their peer group.

Such cultural dilemmas do not affect everyone, of course. Some parents easily let go of their children as they leave home for college, jobs, or create their own families. Many adolescents are not slavish conformers, and many parents of adolescents are flexible in what they expect from their offspring. Many men and women leave their home communities to find jobs and lives elsewhere and never look back, just as many remain attached to their hometowns and feel no regrets about staying there. People respond differently to these dilemmas depending upon their gender, social class, or religious and ethnic background.

Nonetheless, such dilemmas are significant for the culture as a whole, even if not for every participant in it. Perhaps the clearest manifestation of their importance is the fact that they are so often the subject of discourse. That is, people talk about such matters, newspaper columnists write articles about them, social critics and commentators worry about them, members of the clergy sermonize about them, and social scientists construct theories about them. Experts advise parents about how to resolve conflicts with their adolescent children, steering a middle course between too much and too little control. Newspaper editorials condemn the selfishness of yuppies and lament the fact that too few people care about others. Feminists complain that women are assigned too much responsibility for maintaining kinship connections and providing for the emotional needs of men and that they have little opportunity to become individuals or to succeed in highly competitive careers.

These forms of discourse are interesting not because they are true or false, but because of what they tell us about cultural anxieties and dilemmas. Nowhere is this more true than with respect to discourse about self-esteem. When contemporary people speak of self-esteem, they are in part responding to and recreating these and other anxieties and dilemmas. When educators, social scientists, editorial writers, members of the clergy, and others criticize the emphasis on self-esteem and dispute the arguments of the conceptual entrepreneurs, they do the same. Thus, what people say as they espouse and challenge the myth of self-esteem reveals something about the nature of the cultural world they inhabit. And it is this cultural world that energizes both the myth's proponents and its opponents.

We can see the variety of ways in which the myth of self-esteem is part and parcel of American culture by looking more closely at the culture and its inherent contradictions.

SOCIETY AND THE INDIVIDUAL

No word is more indicative of the root ideas—and controversies—of American culture than the word *individual*. It is the individual who is urged to succeed and praised for doing so, and it is in competition with other individuals that he or she must do so. When Americans think of happiness, it is mainly the happiness of the individual they have in mind. "Individuality" is something people are thought to naturally seek and value, for "everybody's different." "Individualism" is a virtue—it is right to stick up for oneself, to be one's own person, to be an "individualist." In education, it is considered a good idea to "individualize" instruction, for each child is said to learn differently and at his or her own pace.

When Americans use the word *individual* they often have in mind a contrast (or even a conflict) between the individual and the larger society. In fact, the very first element in the dictionary definition is "A single human being considered *apart from* a society or community."[3] The individual pursues success on behalf of himself or herself, and any benefit the community or society derive from his or her effort is a desirable result but not the main goal. We often think of individual happiness as something gained in spite of the opposition of others, as when a couple marry for love against the wishes of their families. The individualist is often someone who thumbs his or her nose at society and chooses an unconventional lifestyle.

Upon closer inspection, however, the American preoccupation with the individual is more complex and far less certain than it appears on the surface. It is individuals who succeed, but they and their admirers seldom accept or give praise without attributing at least part of their success to others. In television award shows, for example, when an individual performer receives an Oscar or a Grammy, he or she almost invariably thanks a host of others, from fellow performers and professional associates to family members. Without him, her, or they, the performer asserts, I could not have achieved my success. There is an element of ritual in such acknowledgments, of course, and frequently we question their sincerity. Still, the very fact that people feel obliged to acknowledge the help of others, even if insincerely, indicates that they are answering to values in addition to individualism.

Moreover, "individuality" is not an unqualified good, nor is it always clear just what Americans mean when they refer to it. Generations of American adolescents, for example, have sought to differentiate themselves from their parents, from the adult world in general, and often from one another by adopting distinctive clothing styles and musical tastes. For a time, as a teenager I affected the clothing and demeanor of the "Beat Generation," read Jack Kerouac's *On the Road,* frequented coffeehouses, and generally did all I could to make my parents wonder what they had produced. My own children found their own ways of accomplishing the same end, and in my classes I observe students making similar statements about their individuality. But for all of the supposed individuality these practices signify, they also denote our attachment to others. We differentiate ourselves from some people by slavishly conforming to the fashion or musical or political dictates of others. Individuality seems to require sameness as well as difference. And it surely requires an audience ready to applaud (or condemn) this individuality and agree wholeheartedly about what is good (or bad) about it.

Americans also seem to be capable of emphasizing the "community" over the individual. They may speak of community only with great difficulty, as critics have alleged, or be capable of creating only fragile and short-lived forms of community. Still, there is evidence not only that Americans like many of the features of community but also that in various ways they actually succeed in creating real communities. They tend to speak of the collectivities that are important to them as communities: The neighborhood is a "community" and there are numerous entities such as the "musical community," the "gay community," and the "Jewish community" or the "African-American community." Moreover, Americans not only hold such sentiments of community but also frequently act on them. They join and attend churches at a greater rate than do the members of other societies, and they respond actively and generously to appeals to help the victims of natural disasters.

Finally, there is a basic difference of opinion, perhaps especially in contemporary American culture, about how individuals should define themselves in relation to the social world. Ralph Turner has captured this difference in his discussion of what he calls the "institutional" and "impulsive" forms of self-anchorage.[4] Turner characterizes the institutional form of self-anchorage as one in which the individual finds a sense of his or her "real self" by adhering to social expectations and cultural standards. The institutionally anchored person believes the self is something created by effort and achievement, and that one is being true to oneself when one meets obligations to others, especially when tempted not to do so. In the institutional form, the individual feels his or her real self is revealed when he or she resists the temptation to call in sick in order to enjoy a pleasant spring day or remains faithful to a spouse or partner in spite of the opportunity to stray.

The impulsive form of self-anchorage, in contrast, rests on the belief that each person has a true self that is open to discovery. This self may be suppressed by social conventions or concealed because the person must meet the artificial obligations of social roles. Thus, the impulse-anchored person believes the true self is revealed when the person resists the demand to do what is expected and instead does what he or she truly wants to do. In the impulsive form, the feeling is that if a person wants to call in sick in order to enjoy a fine summer day, then he or she should do so, because to conform and go to work is to deny the true self. And infidelity might be taken as a sign that the real self is breaking through the artificial restraints of propriety.

Thus, words like "individual" and "society" hold different meanings for each of these types. For the institutionally anchored person, "individualism" means doing the right thing, doing what is socially expected and obligatory, thus resisting the temptation to fall short of expectations. For the impulse-anchored person, "individualism" means doing what one truly wants to do, thus resisting demands to conform outwardly to social expectations.

American "individualism" then is a more complex phenomenon than it may superficially appear to be. As Will Wright has shown in his analysis of the Western movie, even the ruggedly independent, individualist cowboy hero has a relationship to the community. The stranger—Shane, for example, of the classic film—appears as if from nowhere and eventually uses his distinctive abilities to save the town from outlaws who threaten its peace. He is an outsider whom the locals do not know and cannot fully accept. Yet, as they discover, he is a skilled gunfighter, and therefore is accorded a special place in the community. Eventually he fights and overcomes the outlaws and makes the community safe. Only then can he be accepted by the community and remain there, if he chooses to do so. In staying, however, the hero must give up his special status and become like others in the community. Shane, like many others, cannot do so, and decides to leave.[5]

This analysis portrays a conflicted relationship between the individual and the social world. Individuality—represented by special skills—is the basis on which one joins a community and makes common cause with others. Yet membership in the community requires that one not make too much of those skills, that one not too strongly claim a special or unique status. One must be different to gain membership, yet be like others to retain it. Like Rudolph the Red-Nosed Reindeer, whose nose lights the way for Santa's sleigh, the individual must have something to offer others, but at the same time those talents have to be fastened to the collective harness!

Where and how does the myth of self-esteem and discourse about self-esteem enter this complex picture of the individual and society? First, it is this culture that provides the impetus for the many ideas and assumptions gathered under the broad umbrella provided by the myth of self-esteem. From William James to the present, the sociologists and psychologists who have contributed the key ideas and findings in the scientific literature on self-esteem have not worked independently of the culture in which they have formed their ideas. Rather, they have seen the individual and society through eyes formed within the culture and by the perspectives it encourages. If culture engenders ambivalent feelings about both individualism and the community, it is likely that social scientists will share this ambivalence, seek to examine it, and sometimes try to resolve it. Cultural definitions of the individual and the society are not the only influences on their ideas, of course, for social scientists strive to develop some degree of autonomy from their culture. They try to ask and answer questions stimulated by their own theoretical concerns, and not only by issues made important in the culture.

Nonetheless, they are influenced by the ideas they have absorbed from their culture and by the issues it forces to their attention. Hence, James, Mead, and the others were in one way or another interested in how individual and society are related, and their theories reflect this concern.

These social theorists, who laid the conceptual foundations for contemporary ideas about self-esteem, were thus answering culturally stimulated questions about the relationship between the individual and the society. How independent can the person be from the surrounding social world? Must there be a relationship of antagonism between the two? How can individuals gain some autonomy from others and still be positively tied to them? The propositions of these social thinkers are answers to these questions, as are the statements of their contemporary followers in the self-esteem movement. Self-esteem, they say, is entirely in the hands of the individual. Most of the obstacles to self-esteem arise from the way society treats the person. People can only think well of themselves if they learn cultural expectations and then develop the competence to meet them. These and similar statements about self-esteem also are general propositions about the nature of the individual and the society.

While social scientists try to achieve some distance from the culture, the conceptual entrepreneurs of self-esteem impose no such limitations on themselves. The sociologist knows it is risky to make assertions about human nature, precisely because they are likely to be shaped by cultural assumptions of which we can easily remain unaware. The self-esteem advocate is more likely to embrace without any qualms or reservations the proposition that self-esteem is a universal human motivation. The entrepreneur with a package of classroom exercises to sell to teachers and school districts has an eye on what potential customers are likely to find appealing. There is no premium for scientific accuracy, and certainly not for a humble and cautious view of the potential efficacy of these exercises. The entrepreneur wants scientific legitimacy for his or her wares, but has neither the time nor inclination to ponder the possibility that the product is really cultural snake oil.

Nor are the potential buyers of these wares keenly alert to their possible limitations or greatly appreciative of truth in advertising. Just as Americans who can afford them are eager to purchase automobiles for the excitement and social status they promise, they are keen to adopt ideas that make promises about self-feeling. In the car buyer's heart of hearts there is perhaps a dim recognition that the excitement will diminish at approximately the same rate as the new car smell disappears, and that the social status conferred by a new Lexus is largely an illusion. Likewise, the self-esteem enthusiast may vaguely recognize that nothing can be as easy as the self-esteem promoters suggest it is, or that feeling good about oneself is not quite the same as self-respect. Even so, the impulse to buy is strong. I love what you do for me, self-esteem!

In other words, American culture creates not only a set of ideas but also a ready market for them. It does so not in spite of the fact that these ideas are often confused and self-contradictory but in large part *because* of the fact. A culture that fosters ambivalence about the proper relationship between the person and the surrounding social world creates a market that is ready to absorb myths about that relationship and is especially eager to do so if these myths cater to that ambivalence. By urging people to believe in themselves and feel that their fate is in their own hands, the myth of self-esteem satisfies that part of American culture that puts the individual on center stage and authorizes his or her priority over others. By emphasizing that everybody is special and deserving of high self-esteem, the myth expresses the same relationship between the person and the society as does the cowboy myth. By urging that the responsibility for developing self-esteem lies with parents and teachers, the myth speaks to the opposite cultural inclinations. And by stressing that self-esteem has positive social consequences, the myth underscores the fact that individuals must contribute their special talents, their self-esteem, to the group.

Self-esteem is also a highly marketable term because its very ambiguity of meaning provides some psychic cover for the ambivalence many people experience as a result of their opposing desires to feel good about and respect themselves. Although this distinction is a matter of intense cultural debate, the existence of the debate is evidence of the deep cultural resonance of the issue. American culture enjoins the pursuit of happiness, and because psychology has increasingly provided the language in which people describe happiness, it has enjoined them to feel good about themselves. But the culture also enjoins people to do those things that will earn them self-respect—not just to feel good about themselves, but to have the sense that they have earned a measure of honor and deference. Given this contradiction, the divergent and ambiguous messages of self-esteem are a blessing for the ambivalent.

The ambiguous messages of the myth of self-esteem do more than satisfy a craving for information about the person, what the person should be like, and how the person should relate to others. These very ideas help perpetuate the craving, even as they are offered as a means of satisfying it. Hence, the myth of self-esteem not only derives from the complexities of American culture but also helps realize them.

How can this be so? The answer lies partly in the same processes whereby consumer goods that offer excitement and status soon lose their capacity to satisfy the needs that advertising has created, and must be replaced. As the new car smell fades and newer, more exciting, higher-status cars appear on the market, the consumer grows dissatisfied and wants the latest model. Likewise, as the latest diet or exercise fad fails to produce the promised results, the consumer looks for something newer and more promising. There is no reason to think that the situation is much different with regard to self-help advice in general and self-esteem in particular. Just as one set of self-affirming statements or motivational techniques becomes obsolete, a new set becomes available to take its place. Conceptual entrepreneurship has found a ready market, stimulated a new set of wants and needs, and is ever-ready to maintain and supply the demand for its products.

There is more to the matter than the restimulation of demand, however, for the myth of self-esteem also relates rather directly to some fundamental ambiguities in Americans' conception of the good life. "Happiness" and "success" are goals toward which Americans are culturally enjoined to strive, but there is by no means wide agreement on what these desirable things really amount to. There are competing definitions of happiness and success, and the myth of self-esteem plays into this competition and helps sustain it.

PURSUING HAPPINESS AND SUCCESS

Along with life and liberty, "the pursuit of happiness" is one of the unalienable rights mentioned in the U. S. Declaration of Independence. This remarkable document does not even begin to tell us what happiness is or how to pursue it, nor during the more than two centuries that have passed since Thomas Jefferson wrote the Declaration have Americans been able to agree on these matters. In a diverse society, happiness can be almost anything one wants it to be. Like beauty, it lies in the eyes of the beholder, whose only certainty is that the pursuit of happiness is an entitlement.

Although the nature of happiness is uncertain, it is possible to discern amidst its many meanings two competing and nearly opposite versions of what it is and how to pursue it. Not surprisingly, these competing definitions are mirrored in the contrasting understandings of self-esteem that I have described.

One American version of happiness is captured in Jefferson's choice of words: the *pursuit* of happiness. Whatever it might be, however it might be defined by the individual or by his or her social groups, happiness is something to be sought. It lies in the future, perhaps just out of reach, perhaps far away, but still attainable. Whether the pursuit demands effort or requires luck, whether happiness consists of wealth or fame or accomplishment, it is a goal that can be won. Whatever its current state, somehow and somewhere there is more of it to be had.

A variety of cultural images support this version of happiness, but one that conveys it well is the story of Dorothy and her compatriots in the Land of Oz. Each seeks the Wizard of Oz for a different purpose—the Cowardly Lion wants courage, the Scarecrow a brain, the Tin Man a heart, and

Dorothy wants to find a way to return to her home in Kansas. Each is really engaged in a quest for the same thing, for a happiness that lies somewhere ahead in some new acquisition or state of being. And it can be attained only if they reach the Emerald City, and can be granted only by the elusive but omnipotent Wizard.

Contemporary Americans seek a variety of Emerald Cities, and their aspirations frequently involve one or another kind of Wizard. For some, happiness lies in becoming thinner or better dressed or more athletic, and wizards assume the varying forms of diet experts, fashion advisors, and fitness trainers. For others, the Emerald City promises a life free of addiction or self-doubt, and the wizards are twelve-step programs or self-esteem gurus promising personal transformation. For still others, happiness is a new job or a new house or a new life in a new location. Whatever happiness is, it inevitably seems to lie elsewhere—on the other side of the fence, the other side of the tracks, the other side of the country, or the other side of the mind.

The story of Dorothy in Oz also tells us, however, about an opposite version of happiness, one that ultimately triumphs in her tale and to some extent ultimately prevails in the real lives most Americans live. Dorothy's compatriots eventually discover that the Wizard is an ordinary person whose powers lie only in the manipulation of special effects, of illusions, from behind his curtain. They discover that they possessed all along the very virtues they sought, that they lacked only the external symbols—a medal to certify the Cowardly Lion's bravery, a symbolic heart for the Tin Man, a diploma to attest to the Scarecrow's intelligence. Dorothy makes the most important discovery of all, that "there's no place like home." She awakens from her dream, safe in her bed, surrounded by familiar faces, secure in her newly found understanding that happiness lies in Kansas, not over the rainbow. It was only a dream!

The belief that "there's no place like home," like the recognition that the grass is really not any greener on the other side of the fence, marks the opposing version of happiness. Those people who are happy, in this version, are content with who and where they are; they come to the understanding that they had all along what they were seeking. Like Dorothy, they learn that they are already happy, and that those who fervently seek happiness may never discover that they already have it. There is no new job, new house, or new life that can provide any better for their happiness. They have discovered that happiness lies in contentment.

Just as there are competing understandings of the nature of happiness, so too there are opposing definitions of success.[6] One version of success emphasizes the acquisition of wealth or fame through some form of individual effort. To be counted a "success" in this version, one must somehow "make one's mark" in the world. Whether the route to success involves selling a product, acquiring wealth through real estate, or developing musical or athletic talent, the meaning of success lies in what the individual gets as a result of being successful. Indeed, the means by which the individual attains success often is counted as less important than the eventual measures of success. As a result, the counterfeit version of fame or celebrity sometimes is valued as much as the real thing, and Americans recognize that stolen money buys the same consumer goods as hard-earned money.

The countervailing notion of success emphasizes accomplishment in a calling and satisfaction in its pursuit. The calling might be an occupational one—from the most skilled profession to the least skilled manual labor—or it might be defined much more broadly. In this version of success, the physician who becomes a beloved family doctor in a small town will be considered as much of a success as the wealthy urban specialist who earns several times as much. The ordinary worker will be encouraged to feel successful by doing as good of a job as possible when digging ditches or delivering mail. And, more broadly, success can be defined as providing for a family, being a good parent, doing good deeds for others in the community, or being a respected member of a church. In this version of success, the extrinsic rewards of wealth and fame are counted as much less important than the intrinsic satisfactions of work and lifestyle. People are encouraged to think of themselves as already successful, or at least as having the means of success within their grasp, rather than urged to seek their fortunes elsewhere or in the future.

Much as contentment triumphs over an idealized future happiness in the story of Dorothy in the Land of Oz, so too what the individual has already achieved often triumphs over aspiration as the measure of success. One of our contemporary American tales of self-reconciliation describes a midlife crisis in which people arriving at middle age are faced with the recognition that they have already built their lives and have achieved as much as they will ever achieve.[7] This recognition is said to frequently precipitate a sense of personal crisis, to which the individual responds unproductively with rebellion, sexual exploits, or the abandonment of a career, home, or family. But in the idealized resolution of this crisis, the individual comes to value the occupational success and way of life he or she has already achieved. Thus, in coming to terms with reality, and perhaps learning to love it, the individual achieves what all regard as a more solid form of success and the variety of happiness we call contentment.

The title character played by Richard Dreyfus in the film *Mr. Holland's Opus* also illustrates this version of success. An aspiring composer, Mr. Holland becomes a high school music teacher in order to pay the bills. With a family to help support, including a deaf son who requires expensive private schooling, he takes on extra teaching duties and finds little time to compose. He gradually becomes a committed and highly successful teacher who is devoted to his students. When forced to retire because of budget cuts, he attends an emotional gathering in his honor. There, his former students form an orchestra that plays the composition on which he has been working for thirty years. Mr. Holland's opus—his life work—is not just that composition, however, as everyone reminds him, but the success and happiness of all of those students whose lives he has touched. He is not a failure, they assure him, but a magnificent success.

The varying meanings of self-esteem cater to and reflect these opposing versions of happiness and success. On the one hand, self-esteem is offered as a means of attaining these goals. Self-esteem, people are assured, will provide the energy, focus, and self-confidence they need to attain happiness and success. But on the other hand, self-esteem also is offered as a goal in itself, indeed as a measure of happiness and success. And, like the Scarecrow's diploma, the basis for self-esteem is said to be something the individual possessed all along, needing only self-acceptance to certify it.

Viewed in the light of these contrasting ideas about happiness and success, the myth of self-esteem tells a familiar cultural story in new words. Versions of the myth that stress the wonderful results of increased self-esteem promise yet another route to success and happiness. There is a sense—and one should not exaggerate here—in which the promise of self-esteem is not unlike the promise of the West a century and a half ago. Then, California and Oregon were places to dream about, places that promised the wealth of gold or the opportunity to claim good land, places to be successful and happy. The quest for self-esteem involves none of the hard work and danger of the Oregon Trail, and in that sense it is an easier journey on which to embark. Like the West, self-esteem attracts not only those whose commitment to self-improvement is sincere and who are ready for hard work, but also those who want to acquire self-esteem (and get rich) more quickly. Just as the great transcontinental migration had its guidebooks and promoters, self-esteem has its own conceptual entrepreneurs.

Versions of the myth of self-esteem that put more emphasis on finding enhanced self-regard in one's own back yard, as it were, also have their counterpart in earlier American stories of success and happiness. Not everyone set out for California; some were content to stay behind in Illinois or Iowa, regretting only that they might never see their children or siblings again.[8] Their modern counterparts reject the quest to be thinner or wealthier, finding contentment in self-acceptance. Their reluctance to change involves a resistance to psychic rather than geographical or social mobility, but it is nonetheless a similar reluctance.

The contemporary myth of self-esteem thus breathes new life and new meaning into the recurring American cultural dilemma of whether one should heed the call of distant opportunity or be content to remain in place. There is an irony here worth mentioning: The myth of self-esteem is often touted as a great discovery, as a new way of providing for individual and social well-being. Likewise, the social scientists who have studied self-esteem have viewed themselves as scientific discoverers charting new truths about human conduct. Yet the myth of self-esteem seems to repeat old cultural "truths." The ideas and findings of psychologists, together with the retail offerings of the conceptual entrepreneurs, become absorbed into older and more deeply rooted cultural tales and traditions.

Thus I am skeptical of fears that the widespread adoption of psychological vocabularies of the self should be viewed as a threat. Ideas about self-esteem do hold considerable power over contemporary Americans, influencing the way we see and present ourselves. And the purveyors of these ideas, both wholesale and retail, likewise hold some power. But their ideas do not fully reshape the psychology of Americans, for they become entangled with and in some ways absorbed into existing cultural myths.

AGAINST SELF-ESTEEM

The prominence of self-esteem in the contemporary vocabulary of self might easily lead one to think that everybody believes in its curative powers. This is not so, however, as a variety of voices have almost from the beginning been raised against the myth of self-esteem. Newspaper columnists and social commentators have criticized and sometimes ridiculed the self-esteem movement. The California Commission was the target of cartoonist Gary Trudeau's biting satire in *Doonesbury* and provoked the ire of conservative critics of government. Educational critics, parents, and even some educators have sounded alarms about the dangers of self-esteem theory in the schools. Signs of a cultural backlash against self-esteem are everywhere, and a recent spate of critical books suggests that the concept may have already reached its high-water mark.

How should we interpret resistance to the myth of self-esteem? One interpretation would hold that the myth has been or is being exposed, that its promises to solve social problems and provide for individual happiness and profit are being revealed as false. According to this logic, self-esteem is a bad idea whose time has come and gone. Soon, we might expect, conceptual entrepreneurs will turn their energies to the marketing of new panaceas. Their discoveries about self-esteem discredited by science, they will seek new solutions to our problems. New forms of snake oil will replace outmoded ones.

The recurring appeal of ideas similar to the myth of self-esteem makes me wary of such an interpretation. Although self-esteem may be on the wane as an explanation of human behavior and as a tool for solving pressing social problems, this development has as little to do with scientific findings or evidence as did the spread of the myth in the first place. After all, in the past, proponents of self-esteem have had little difficulty maintaining their beliefs in the face of contradictory scientific evidence. And even though such criticism may spell the demise of self-esteem as a social theory, the critics are themselves no more interested in scientific evidence than the proponents. The critics knew it was snake oil all along, and the believers still believe, even if in the future they may be less vocal about their convictions. The rise and possible decline of self-esteem seems to be more than a case of a false theory refuted or a bogus discovery revealed.

But what more is it? The answer to this question is that criticism of the myth of self-esteem is a manifestation of the very divisions in American culture that we have just considered. The myth of self-esteem is the object of powerful faith and the topic of strenuous argument because those who promote it and those who oppose it are moved by impulses that spring from deeper sources than they imagine. Both the faithful and the heretics are, in a sense, spokespersons for the disagreements that are endemic to American culture, which no scientific evidence could possibly resolve.

Nowhere has the theory of self-esteem generated more controversy than in education. Here, where the theory is most strongly expressed and persistently transformed into practice, there has been continuing and fervent opposition. For critics of contemporary education, the self-esteem theory and the educational practices to which it gives rise threaten to reduce already low standards of achievement. The "rising tide of mediocrity," one conservative critic writes, is now "being swelled by another huge wave: a tsunami of artificial self-esteem."[9] Another argues that the self-esteem movement forces teachers to "accept every child as is." To criticize children in any way, or to give them tasks at which they might not succeed, such as difficult homework or even a test, is to risk damaging their self-esteem. The result of this tendency to treat each child "like a fragile therapy consumer in constant need of an ego boost" is a lowering of educational standards.[10] Where the "self-esteem movement" holds sway in education, critics argue, students are graded too generously, no one can fail, and, as one writer puts it, ". . . standards are not based on what students should do, or are able to do, but on what they will do, no matter how low the common denominator."[11]

Critics of the self-esteem theory make two key distinctions when they specify the grounds for their opposition. First, they argue that contemporary educational theorists and teachers fail to distinguish between self-*esteem* and self-*respect*. Self-esteem, they say, means self-liking, whereas self-respect means the capacity to accept tough challenges and deal with the possibility of failure. Columnist William Raspberry puts it this way:

> Unlike dignity, which can be accorded even to the unde-
> serving, or self-esteem, which can thrive on the sugary

diet of self-affirmation ("I am a good person"), self-
respect is both an acknowledgment of personal responsibility and an assertion of one's ability to meet that responsibility.[12]

It is self-respect and not self-esteem, critics say, that teachers should strive
to foster in their students. And it is achievement and not groundless self-
approval that they should encourage.

The second, and closely related distinction, is between *earned* and
learned self-esteem. The problem, critics say, is that educational theory mis-
takenly believes that self-esteem can be taught and therefore learned. Self-
esteem, they assert, cannot be so easily attained. Rather, it must be acquired
the old-fashioned way: one must *earn* it. An elementary school educator
and critic whose views have been widely cited and reprinted puts it this
way:

Like it or not, self-esteem is very much a function of such
unyielding realities as what we can do, what we've done
with what we have and what we've made of ourselves.[13]

Self-esteem, say the critics, is a *result* of educational accomplishment, not a
substitute for real education.

While for many educators self-esteem is the source of all good, then for
many critics it is just as certainly the root of all evil, particularly the evil of
narcissism. In a formulation that ironically reverses the proponents' claims
for the good consequences of high self-esteem, one author explains that the
sort of self-esteem favored in the schools provides only "momentary plea-
sures," not happiness. In the long run, children taught this way will be restless and dissatisfied, constantly turning to "drugs, alcohol, irresponsible
sexuality, and crime." For these activities ". . . promise the satisfactions that
self-esteem seekers are looking for, and they promise them now: instant
pleasure, instant relief, instant success."[14] Unearned self-esteem not only
lowers academic standards, it seems, but also renders the young prone to
the very temptations—drugs, irresponsible sex, and crime—that advocates
of self-esteem would claim it insulates them against.

Opposition to self-esteem in education stems in part from the same
sources as does a more general critique of education. That is, from the vantage point of educational critics, the schools are generally not very successful in teaching skills and producing responsible citizens, and self-esteem
becomes part of the critics' explanation of this failure. From the vantage
point of religious and cultural conservatives, by teaching self-esteem the
schools are undermining traditional values of hard work and personal
responsibility, as well as poaching on what is regarded as the rightful
province of the family and of religious institutions.

At the same time, this opposition makes use of the various dimensions of self-esteem's meaning that I presented earlier, and it takes part in more general cultural debates. Thus, for example, critics worry that the educational theory of self-esteem puts too much emphasis on the individual and too little on social responsibility. They are concerned that this form of instruction makes too few demands on the individual, essentially reassuring children that they need not change or improve in order to have higher self-esteem. They argue that self-esteem is only meaningful if it leads to some good result—that feeling good about oneself is not enough—and that self-esteem is *really* self-respect, not feeling good.

Critics of the self-esteem movement outside of education similarly express positions that reaffirm one pole or another of the opposing meanings of self-esteem or the divergent poles of American culture more generally. The well-known child development psychologist William Damon takes strong issue with the movement.[15] One of the most important "misconceptions of modern times," in his view, is the "elevation of self," and one of its worst effects is the misguided emphasis on the child's self-esteem. Damon grounds his critique partly in what he properly regards as the misuse (or sheer ignorance) of scientific research into self-esteem by enthusiasts. Citing Ruth Wylie's massive compilation of self-esteem studies, which showed generally that the preponderance of studies either do not support or contradict popular ideas about self-esteem, he also points to problems in the measurement of self-esteem which in his opinion make the very general measures of self-esteem usually employed almost useless.[16]

Underlying his scientific critique, however, is a conception of self-esteem that differs significantly from what many movement advocates propose. For Damon, self-esteem is not grounded in feeling good about oneself, but in competence. Thus, efforts to enhance children's self-esteem are misdirected, and we would ". . . do better to help children acquire the skills, values, and virtues on which a positive sense of self is properly built."[17] Using words like "competence" and "character," Damon argues that children have to learn to cope with stubborn realities, be held to consistent standards, and that they must learn ". . . a deep and abiding respect for others in their lives."[18] He argues strongly that self-esteem, like happiness, cannot be an end in itself. It is a product of correct ways of bringing up children and of their being held to standards and provided with guidance, and emphasizing the child's self-consciousness by focusing on a quest for self-esteem can in the end only interfere with their self-esteem.

Another recent critic of the self-esteem movement, William B. Swann, a psychologist who has extensively studied the phenomenon, argues that self-esteem cannot be acquired as easily as the enthusiasts believe.[19] Supporters of the self-esteem movement wrongly assume, he says, that people have an overwhelming desire to feel good about themselves. Although this may be true on some level, people also have a desire to act and think consistently with their images of themselves. One result is that people with low self-esteem find it difficult to act or think in ways that would improve their self-esteem, for to do so would be to violate an existing self-image. Moreover, those with low self-esteem feel unentitled to praise, and tend to resist it or feel uneasy about it when it is received. As a result, the methods recommended by the self-esteem movement are ineffective or counterproductive.

More crucially, he says, self-esteem is not simply a matter of individual belief or preference. Individual self-esteem is shaped by the person's involvement in a network of social relationships and by his or her commitment to culturally sponsored beliefs and activities. At the interpersonal level, others with whom we have negotiated various relationships may be resistant to our efforts to improve our self-esteem, because their self-images and relationships with us may depend on our continuing to think ill of ourselves. Swann cites the example of a woman who works outside of the home and who resists her husband's becoming a "househusband," because even though it makes him feel better it makes her feel worse about her own career involvements and "neglect" of household activities. At a cultural level, Swann says, people pursue such ideals as romantic love or the goal of career success, but often these activities put them into positions where they cannot think better of themselves. Romantic love leads to relationships that demean some individuals, and where everything is staked on success or the economic rewards of success, self-esteem may never be attained. In short, the individual is enmeshed in a social world that may make attaining self-esteem a difficult and lengthy task, not an easy matter of self-redefinition.

Damon and Swann, who are among the most articulate of critical voices raised against self-esteem, make a serious effort to ground their condemnation in scientific understandings of the self. Yet in some sense their animus against the self-esteem movement appears to spring from deeper cultural sources. Their conclusions are objective, to be sure, and by and large I regard them as far more sound than the beliefs of those who adhere to the myth of self-esteem. Yet they are moved by convictions about what people should be and should do that stem from ideas of competence, the individual's involvement in and dependence upon the social world, and social standards of virtue and right conduct.

Critics of self-esteem may prefer to see themselves as defenders of an endangered cultural tradition, perhaps the only responsible people standing between this tradition and its demise. But the fact that psychologists express such ideas and find scientific support for them is evidence that such convictions have not been supplanted by the myth of self-esteem. Likewise, the fact that there are critics who decry the ascendancy of self-esteem in education is evidence that ideas of social responsibility, competence, and standards of conduct have not disappeared. The critics exist, in part, because that part of the American cultural tradition persists, I suspect, rather than being the cause of its persistence. They are a part of a cultural debate about the nature of success and happiness, the responsibilities and freedoms of the individual, the claims society may and may not make of individuals.

WHAT IS SELF-ESTEEM, REALLY?

The multiple meanings and uses of self-esteem and the existence of cultural debates and polarities in which those who espouse or oppose self-esteem participate, intentionally or not, raises a final question: Is there anything real about self-esteem? Is it only a myth that serves a variety of particular needs or purposes? Is it only snake oil?

In the next and final chapter I turn to these questions. Just as the preceding chapters have asked readers to suspend belief in the myth of self-esteem, Chapter 6 will require that suspension of belief to be maintained. Even more, it will ask the reader to entertain quite a different way of thinking about self-esteem. I cannot promise definitive answers to these questions, of course, but I can promise interesting and provocative ones.

NOTES

1. This discussion of culture is indebted to Kai T. Erikson, *Everything in Its Path* (New York: Simon and Schuster, 1976); see also Anne Swidler, "Culture in Action: Symbols and Strategies." *American Sociological Review* 51, 1986: 273–286.
2. John P. Hewitt, *Dilemmas of the American Self.* Philadelphia: Temple University Press, 1989.
3. *The American Heritage Electronic Dictionary,* emphasis added.
4. Ralph H. Turner, "The Real Self: From Institution to Impulse." *American Journal of Sociology* 81, March 1976: 989–1016.
5. See Will Wright, *Six Guns and Society: A Structural Study of the Western.* Berkeley: University of California Press, 1975.
6. See, for example Rex Burns, *Success in America: The Yeoman Dream and the Industrial Revolution.* Amherst: University of Massachusetts Press, 1976.
7. The cultural classics on this topic include Daniel J. Levinson, *The Seasons of a Man's Life* (New York: Knopf, 1978) and Gail Sheehy, *Passages: Predictable Crises of Adult Life* (New York: Dutton, 1976). More recently, Sheehy has written another entry in this genre. See her

New Passages: Mapping Your Life across Time (New York: Random House, 1995).

8. See Lewis O. Saum, *The Popular Mood of Pre-Civil War America.* Westport, Conn.: Greenwood, 1980.

9. Chester E. Finn Jr., "Narcissus Goes to School." *Commentary* 69, June 1990: 40.

10. John Leo, "The Trouble with Self-Esteem." *U. S. News and World Report* 108, April 2, 1990: 16.

11. Mike Schmoker, "Self-Esteem Is Earned, Not Learned." *Los Angeles Times* 108, October 7, 1989: II–8.

12. Raspberry, William. "Self-Esteem or Self-Respect?" *The Washington Post* 113, April 16, 1990: A15.

13. Schmoker, op. cit., II–8.

14. Barbara Lerner, "Student Self-Esteem and Academic Excellence." *Education Digest* 52, September 1986: 34.

15. William Damon, *Greater Expectations: Overcoming the Culture of Indulgence in America's Homes and Schools.* New York: Free Press, 1995.

16. Ruth Wylie, *The Self-Concept: Theory and Research on Selected Topics.* Lincoln: University of Nebraska Press, 1979, 690, as cited in Damon, op. cit., 75.

17. Damon, op. cit., 72.

18. Ibid., 79.

19. William B. Swann Jr., *Self-Traps: The Elusive Quest for Higher Self-Esteem.* New York: W. H. Freeman, 1996.

6

The Reality of Self-Esteem

S elf-esteem is the center of a powerful mythology, but it is not merely an empty word that signifies nothing. The proponents of self-esteem are mistaken in their faith in its capacity to guarantee individual happiness and solve social problems, but indirectly and perhaps unwittingly they have grasped something of importance about the psychology of contemporary people. Opponents are correct in their skepticism about claims made on behalf of self-esteem, but they are mistaken in dismissing the phenomenon out of hand. Self-esteem has a social and psychological reality, and my task in this final chapter is to explore it.

My purpose is not to adjudicate between the proponents and opponents of self-esteem or between alternative definitions of what self-esteem is or how to get it. The arguments and differences of meaning we have examined represent disagreements about what the social world should be like and how people should behave. They are not resolvable by scientific evidence or theory. My purpose is to develop an alternative perspective on self-esteem, a way of looking at the phenomenon that sheds a new and perhaps unexpected light on it.

IS SELF-ESTEEM UNIVERSAL?

I begin this task by addressing a key question, namely whether self-esteem is the universal phenomenon that its proponents claim it to be. My skepticism about self-esteem might lead you to expect my answer to be an unequivocal "no," but the question does not lend itself to a simple answer. Self-esteem, we will see, is both universal and culturally specific, hence it is both reality and myth. Its proponents think they have discovered something that they have in reality invented. But their invention of self-esteem and its incorporation as a key element of the American psyche is possible only because of universal features of human nature.

Self-esteem is universal in the same way that the self is universal; to understand the reality of the former we must grapple with the reality of the latter. What is universal about the self and what is culturally shaped? How is the experience of the self different from one culture to another and how is it the same? And how is self-esteem related to the more general concept of the self?

Is the self a universal human experience or phenomenon? The answer depends in part upon how we define our terms. If by "self" we mean something very much like the ideas and beliefs Americans have in mind when they use this term, then the answer is essentially "no." Human cultures have created a variety of ideas about the nature and importance of individuals, the relationship between the individual and society, what motivates people, and where individuals acquire their capacities or traits. Most contemporary Americans tend to believe that the individual has a distinctive if not unique self that sets him or her apart from others. A traditional member of the Hopi people of Arizona, however, would find this a foreign and rather unpleasant way of thinking, taking the view that the person is a member of a people who have found their way to this earth and can find fulfillment only by pursuing traditional cultural practices.[1]

If by self, however, we mean *reflexivity*—the capacity of human beings to be the object of their own thoughts, feelings, and actions—then the answer is clearly "yes." The contemporary yuppie obsessed with acquiring and displaying wealth and status and the traditional Hopi immersed in a community that measures the individual by his or her participation in the "Hopi way" both possess the human propensity for reflexivity. They share the capacity to think about themselves, attach feelings to themselves, and become the object of their own actions. They also share the means of acquiring reflexivity. Both grasp themselves indirectly by seeing themselves from what they imagine to be the perspectives of others—not only the specific others with whom they interact but the community as a whole of which they are a part and the gods or spirits in which they believe.

Both the yuppie and the Hopi have the capacity to recognize themselves as individuals and to imagine how they measure up to the standards of the community and its culture. Both can formulate goals for themselves, be satisfied or dissatisfied with themselves, and reward or punish themselves for success or failure. Both have the capacity for self-consciously governing conduct in accordance with the standards of the group. Both have the capacity to disregard or disobey these standards. The cultural expectations that apply to yuppies and Hopis are very different, of course, for the former is expected to strive for individual success and distinction, whereas the latter is expected to immerse himself or herself in a communal way of life. But each is a reflexive creature.

The experience of reflexivity—however culture shapes the content or nature of the self—is both cognitive and affective. The social world provides the social groups, situations, roles, and social acts within which people experience reflexivity. People see themselves as holding up their end of a conversation, meeting the responsibilities of parenthood, having fun at a party, or being members of a committee or social class. Culture provides people with not only a vocabulary of terms with which to label themselves but also with a set of ideas about human nature, a ready-made discourse about human wants and needs that permits them to interpret their self-experiences.

Human beings also respond affectively—with feeling—to the surrounding world and to themselves. They are bored or elated by conversations, love or resent their children, feel proud or ashamed of their accomplishments. Moreover, they do not merely see themselves as they think others see them, but respond positively or negatively to the real or imagined evaluative responses of others. They are satisfied or disappointed in what they see in themselves, they love or despise themselves, they feel sad about or elated with themselves. They are capable of a variety of emotions directed toward themselves—such as pride, shame, honor, love, guilt—the experience of which is shaped both by the particulars of culture and the universal features of the human experience.[2]

The reality of self-esteem lies in the fact that it is one of these self-referential emotions. Like other such emotions, it depends crucially, but not entirely, on culture. Like all emotions, reflexive ones depend on the vocabulary of emotions the culture makes available. We experience most keenly and fully that which we can name and talk about. We can experience self-esteem, in other words, only if we have a name for it, just as we can experience pride or shame only because we have names for these emotions.

Like all emotions, self-esteem also involves neurological, muscular, visceral—in short, bodily—responses and sensations that are precipitated by human experiences. The grief that contemporary Americans feel over the death of a parent or spouse, for example, involves depressed energy, feelings of being lost or hopeless, intense sadness, crying, and other feeling states that are bodily and not merely "mental." Just as the fact of death is a universal human experience, some of the intense bodily feelings it precipitates probably also have a universal character. This is not to say that all human beings experience grief in this situation. Rather, they have some common bodily, affective reactions that our culture elaborates into what we call grief. Other cultures call the same or similar bodily states by other names, experiencing them as illness, for example, and elaborate a different set of meanings and activities.

The idea that self-esteem is likewise a culturally named emotion is novel and will meet vociferous objection from some quarters. Those convinced of the importance of self-esteem will especially resist categorizing it in this way, for they view it as a universal fact of human nature, not a cultural invention. Nonetheless, by viewing self-esteem as an emotion, we can gain a better grasp of its significance and contemporary meaning.

SELF-ESTEEM AS AN EMOTION

As a beginning point for viewing self-esteem as an emotion, I ask the reader to imagine an analogy with the emotion we commonly call "love." Like self-esteem, love is an elusive feeling, subject to a variety of definitions and to some disagreement about its importance or desirability. Those who are in love generally have no difficulty recognizing the fact, even if they cannot define what love is. Just as self-esteem is often associated with feelings of exuberance or energy, love is associated with feelings of breathless excitement, heart palpitations, and sexual arousal. People seek love, just as they do self-esteem, though they may believe they will never find it or that they do not deserve it. Experts on love offer pronouncements on how to find it, or how to "do" it, just as self-esteem experts offer advice. Love is, in short, a socially constructed emotion—a name for a state of being that involves powerful feelings, renders intense bodily experiences meaningful, and provides people with motives and explanations for their actions. So is self-esteem.

Both self-esteem and love resemble other human emotions, for each consists of a culturally significant and relatively standardized *interpretation* of a set of *feelings* that are aroused in various situations. The feelings associated with emotions take many different forms, depending on the circumstances in which the person finds himself or herself. Under conditions of threat or danger, for example, the individual feels highly mobilized to act, whether by fleeing or fighting. Bodily processes not immediately relevant to survival—such as digestion—slow down or shut down, and the body's resources are directed to the task of meeting the threat. Pulse and respiration speed up, and the body receives an extra supply of adrenalin.

The human experience of emotions associated with such arousal—fear and anger—is not dictated simply by physiological events. There is always a process of interpretation that occurs before, during, and after the arousal of such feelings, and the emotion consists of *both* the feelings *and* the interpretation of them. The belief that one *might* be in danger, as for example when one is alone at night in a place where people have been mugged, is sufficient to produce the physiological arousal we associate with fear. The arousal in turn shapes the way one interprets events—noises and shadows take on new significance, for example, when we believe they may signify that someone is about to attack us. And if one breaks into a run, determined to escape the perceived danger, the experience of fear—which is the named emotion associated with this situation—is as much a result of the activity of running as it is a cause of it. Although we say that we run because we are afraid, it is the act of running from danger that leads us to label our emotional state as fear.

Emotions, then, consist of interpreted physiological or bodily changes. A variety of situations provoke the individual not only to grasp cognitively what is happening so appropriate actions may be taken but also to be affected physiologically in various ways. Sometimes, as in situations that provoke fear, the physiological response is essentially one of arousal or mobilization for action. At other times, the response is nearly the opposite of arousal. The death of a loved one, for example, can provoke a profound depression—that is, an inability or unwillingness to act, a sense of lethargy that makes even physical movement difficult. Whatever the physiological response to a situation, individuals must ordinarily perform actions and interpret their own responses and feelings. We account for the quickened heartbeat in part by calling it "fear" and by associating this emotion with a course of action, perhaps running away. We account for the feeling of dullness and lethargy by calling it "sadness" or "grief" and by associating it with the actions we call mourning.

What are the situations associated with self-esteem, and what kinds of physiological arousal do they produce? There are a variety of ways one might go about answering this question, but the one I will develop here strikes me as a promising and useful way of thinking about self-esteem. It can be stated simply as follows: Self-esteem is interpreted mood. That is, self-esteem is a culturally specific emotion associated with a general human affective response that we can call *mood*.

Mood is a generalized human response to success and failure. All of the diverse situations in which human beings find themselves have an impact on mood. Those situations in which people successfully achieve their goals (or even exceed them) encourage a state of *euphoria*, which is the positive pole of mood. Euphoria entails feelings of energy, alertness, generalized well-being, and an eagerness to face whatever situation next occurs. Situations in which people fail to achieve their goals or fall short of them promote *dysphoria*, which involves a lack of energy, hesitancy to act, and feelings of anxiety, depression, and generalized gloom. Mood ordinarily falls somewhere between these poles. People are seldom either completely dysphoric or euphoric, but rather react to situations in proportion to their degree of success or failure.

Mood, like any other affective response, is experienced when it is named, interpreted, and associated with a line of conduct. It is, therefore, difficult to define mood without using words that themselves provide interpretations of it. Euphoria is not equivalent to "energy" or "well-being," for these are words we use to interpret the feeling. Rather, euphoria is an underlying feeling that is brought into conscious focus by words such as these. Likewise, dysphoria is not equivalent to "gloom" or "sadness," but rather is a state that people interpret and thus experience through these words.

From an evolutionary perspective, we can think of mood as a built-in reward and protection system. That is, successful action is rewarded not only by the results of that action-earning a good grade as a result of studying hard for an examination, for example—but by the positive mood that success promotes. The positive mood reinforces the actions that led to success, and in so doing it encourages the individual to do more of the same. By the same token, the negative mood that occurs as a result of failure operates as a protective mechanism, for it tends to inhibit actions that have led to failure and in so doing keeps the individual out of further difficulty.

Like any kind of human feeling, mood tends to be consciously associated with various lines of conduct and to draw meaning from the actions with which it is associated and the names we give to it. In other words, culture provides both names and courses of action that we can associate with mood, just as it provides names and courses of action we associate with other feelings. The question, then, is how do we name this dimension of human experience and what actions do we associate with it? Self-esteem is part of the answer, but as we will see, only a part.

It seems unlikely that such a general response as mood would have only one name. Every human situation in one way or another involves goals and expectations; sometimes they are met and sometimes they are not. The employee follows the rules and works hard, only to find that his or her job has been eliminated through corporate downsizing. An indifferent student does poorly on an examination but earns an "A" in the course because the professor made an arithmetical mistake in calculating the grade. An imaginary future Boston Red Sox team actually makes it to the World Series and wins, and the incredulous fans exult. A medical researcher spends years in the laboratory perfecting a vaccine and earns fame and fortune as a result. Each of these situations surely has an impact on what we have called mood, but people are apt to interpret these experiences in different ways, with self-esteem being only sometimes a part of the interpretation.

Moreover, cultures differ markedly from one another in the ways they explain or interpret success or failure. The Puritan immigrant to New England in the 1630s, for example, was determined to build a new and more godly community in the American wilderness and was keenly interested in the fate of his or her soul. Convinced that human beings were inherently sinful, Puritans also believed that some were predestined for salvation, and they scrutinized themselves and their experiences intently for signs that they might be among the elect. While Puritans certainly had the fundamental human response we have labeled as mood, they interpreted their feelings with reference to sin and salvation, not self-esteem. It is the contemporary corporate employee carrying the cultural burden of individual responsibility who, feeling depressed or demoralized because of the loss of a job, may interpret the feeling in terms of self-esteem.

Mood, in short, lends itself to a variety of interpretations, and these are shaped both by general cultural ideas and expectations and by the way the culture encourages people to interpret specific experiences. It is American culture generally, we will see, that frequently transforms mood into the self-referential emotion we call self-esteem. It is the actions of conceptual entre-preneurs operating within that cultural framework that give self-esteem its particular meanings. And it is a more particular set of cultural understand-ings that sometimes employ self-esteem as an interpretation of mood and sometimes employ other terms.

SELF-ESTEEM AND THE CULTURE OF INDIVIDUALISM

Viewing self-esteem as a named emotion that provides a culturally relevant and appropriate interpretation of mood gives us a novel way of under-standing self-esteem. There is nothing new or unexpected, however, in the assertion that self-esteem rests upon a foundation of individualism. It is the tendency to place the individual on center stage and to believe that the indi-vidual possesses a distinctive self that makes an emphasis on self-esteem possible. However, self-esteem is not the only interpretation of mood that a culture of individualism could create; thus we must raise and answer a number of questions: What are the alternatives to self-esteem as an inter-pretation of personal experience? Are they the same alternatives that existed a century ago or two centuries ago? If they are not, why has the change occurred? Does the change in vocabulary indicate a major change in the experience of self? What shapes our choice of self-esteem versus other pos-sible interpretations of feelings?

The English language makes available many words individuals can use to interpret the positive or negative feelings that result from success or fail-ure. Having achieved fame, obtained a good grade, or won the lottery, a person might describe himself or herself as happy, joyful, glad, blessed, or fortunate, or some combination of these and similar adjectives. Likewise, the person who has encountered failure might speak of being dejected, unhappy, sad, unlucky, or cursed. Words such as these are self-referential, for they attempt to capture something of the personal meaning of a partic-ular experience. They also frequently mix an interpretation of an emotional state with an explanation of the event that has caused it. To say one is happy to have succeeded describes the emotion one is experiencing; to say one is lucky or blessed is to explain why something has occurred to make one experience this emotion. And just as the individual might make such statements about himself or herself, so others might make such statements about the individual.

There is another array of terms that might be applied, both by individuals experiencing a feeling state and those who observe them doing so. One can imagine an individual saying "I am proud of myself," or "I feel that I have proven my worth." Assertions of pride, self-respect, dignity, value, or self-satisfaction are clearly self-referential. They also contain implicit explanations of success: to be "proud" is to claim credit for an accomplishment as much as to describe the feelings one is experiencing. One can imagine others using these terms as well, but also applying a related set of labels with more negative connotations. Egotism, vanity, narcissism, and conceit come to mind as words others sometimes use to give a negative cast to feelings people themselves describe in positive terms.

People likewise have an array of terms with which to characterize their own and others' dysphoric feelings. They use such general expressions as depression, gloom, dejection, sadness, and unhappiness to describe and explain feelings. And pride and similar terms have their counterparts in modesty, humility, diffidence, reticence, self-hatred, and self-restraint. Each of these words, like those mentioned previously, both describe the emotions the individual is experiencing and provide a way for others to make their own interpretations.

One pair of terms deserves special mention. "Pride" is one of the most common terms people use to express the euphoria that stems from success; "shame" is its dysphoric counterpart. To fall short of one's individual expectations is typically to fall short also of cultural expectations or the expectations of specific other people. To lose a job or fail a test is not merely to fall short of an individual goal, but to fail to live up to one's obligations to others. A common response to such failure is to be *ashamed* at having failed in one's responsibilities, just as to be *proud* is a common response to success.

But just how common are these responses? Are all Americans (or all human beings) always ashamed when they fall short of expectations and proud when they meet them? Or are they sometimes ashamed and sometimes sad, sometimes proud and sometimes happy? And what are the differences between sadness and shame, or pride and happiness? Do such different words merely provide alternative ways for individuals to describe and experience themselves? Or, in contrast, do such differing words and the emotional experiences they make possible have significant consequences for individuals and for the society in which they live?

All of the words mentioned describe self-referential emotions. Pride and shame, however, seem to have a reference outside the individual that appears lacking in such words as sadness and happiness. To say "I am happy to have succeeded" or "I am depressed that I failed" is to define one's emotional experience almost entirely with reference to oneself. *I* am the person experiencing this emotion, these statements seem to assert. To say "I am proud" or "I am ashamed," in contrast, is to associate the emotion one is experiencing with the expectations and responses of others. To be proud is not only to interpret one's emotional state but also to link it to the related emotional states of others, for one can hardly be proud without imagining an audience that is also proud of one. Likewise, one is not only ashamed, but conscious that others are ashamed of one.

Both happiness and pride (or sadness and shame) involve a real or imagined audience, but the individual's relationship with the audience seems to differ. To say, for example, "I'm happy that I got the promotion" is to ask others to approve of or applaud one's happiness and to invite their identification with one. It is the emotional state itself—the individual's happiness—that forms the main basis of the social bond between the happy person and his or her audience. To say, "I'm proud of my promotion" is also to ask for approval and invite identification, but there is more to the social bond than the individual's feeling of pride. The proud person and the approving audience are bound together not only by the emotion, but by a shared sense of the standards or expectations on which it is based.

Some emotional states, then, seem better able than others to foster connections with people. Pride and shame build stronger social ties than happiness and sadness. But who uses which words, and under what circumstances?

HAS THE SELF DECLINED OR DISAPPEARED?

One possible answer to this question is that an emotional vocabulary laden with terms such as "pride" and "shame" (and "self-respect" and "humility") has gradually been giving way to a vocabulary in which words like "self-esteem" and "happiness" are most often used. A century or more ago, according to this view, people had a very different relationship to the social order than they do now. The nature of that difference is well-captured in Ralph Turner's distinction between institutional and impulsive self-anchorage, which was discussed in the previous chapter. Then, people defined themselves in terms of societal standards and felt true to themselves when they could take pride in meeting them. Now, the argument runs, people look within themselves for self-definition and feel true to themselves—or feel happy—by following their own inclinations, not doing what others expect or demand. The institutionally anchored person experienced self through an emotional vocabulary that heavily emphasized pride, self-respect, humility, and shame. The impulsively anchored person experiences an emotional self through such contemporary words as happiness, self-esteem, joy, and depression.

This hypothesis of a sea change in emotional vocabularies in the last century or so is part of a larger set of ideas about changes in the self. Turner's hypothesis of a change from institutional to impulsive forms of self-definition is only one of the ideas that have been advanced by social scientists, historians, and social critics in the last half century to account for perceived changes in American life. Almost fifty years ago, sociologist David Riesman perceived a change from what he and his associates called *inner-directed* to *other-directed* character. Inner-directed individuals learn a set of standards and goals early in life and are thereafter guided by them as though by an internal compass or gyroscope. Other-directed persons are keenly sensitive to the expectations of other people, and they are guided not by a compass but by a psychological radar that tunes them into these expectations.[3]

Later in the 1950s and almost continuously since then, writers have found a variety of ways to describe similar changes in the way Americans experience themselves. Some argued that American culture, which once provided individuals with a clearly defined sense of identity, had gradually made it difficult to do so, with the result that people suffer from a variety of disorders of identity or must constantly engage in a quest for identity. Others argued that Americans had become increasingly selfish or narcissistic, or that the self, which was once solid and robust, had weakened and shrunk. The titles of their books—*The Quest for Identity, The Collective Search for Identity, The Culture of Narcissism, The Minimal Self*—themselves suggest the nature of this diagnosis.[4]

It is tempting to jump on this explanatory bandwagon and regard the growing emphasis on self-esteem as merely another manifestation of this change. The word does have profoundly individualistic implications. Its common usage does seem to emphasize the approval of others, regardless of whether it is earned or is based on any standards of accomplishment. The sense of entitlement associated with self-esteem does suggest a kind of selfishness, for individuals are often urged to pursue their self-esteem without regard for others. And self-esteem also may imply a form of narcissism or a minimal self, in the sense that it provides a skimpy and socially disconnected means of self-definition. Certainly an emphasis on self-esteem as "feeling good about oneself" provides no firm social identity grounded in relationships with others with whom one shares values.

Taken to an extreme, in fact, the apparent popularity of the myth of self-esteem could be taken as a sign that all sorts of bad things have happened to the self. If people define themselves and seek self-esteem only by looking inside themselves, and connect to the social world only by a sense of alienation from it, then in a certain sense they do not have selves at all. The worst fears of the critics of narcissism would seem confirmed. Or, if we adopt an alternative criticism, that the self has come to be governed by those who create the language by means of which we experience it, things do not look any better. From this vantage point, the problem is not individualism or narcissism, but the fact that those who create our vocabularies of self exercise a subtle and unseen form of power over us. They get us to do their bidding by constructing our motives, by getting us to control ourselves as they would have us behave.

Let us not be so quick, however, to adopt this dismal perspective. I cannot settle here the issue of whether the self has changed or declined in the ways critics have charged, but there are reasons to doubt that things are as bad as they seem. Viewing self-esteem as interpreted mood enables me to portray it and its social consequences in a very different light from that ordinarily presented by supporters and critics alike. To do that, I must first discuss my doubts about their analyses.

PUBLIC AND PRIVATE MEANINGS

One major reason to be skeptical of such a gloomy portrayal of the contemporary self lies precisely in the fact that self-esteem has so many meanings. If there were widespread agreement on its meaning—and especially if that meaning were the one intended by many of the conceptual entrepreneurs—then there might be cause for alarm. For in its purest expressions, the myth of self-esteem does encourage a socially disconnected, solipsistic, narcissistic experience of self. However, there is not such agreement, but rather evidence that the word takes on as many familiar meanings as it provides new ones. Proponents of the myth talk about self-esteem as "feeling good about oneself," but the word in use has other meanings—self-respect, pride, happiness, satisfaction, identification with an ethnic group. And the very fact that there is explicit disagreement about the meaning of self-esteem is reason enough to be skeptical that the psychologists and the conceptual entrepreneurs have succeeded in re-engineering the self.

Self-esteem also may be to some extent a linguistic fad, a word that comes into common use for a time and then disappears into cultural oblivion. The widespread use of the concept in education, the frequency of its appearance in advice books and articles, and its use by talk show hosts and guests may be misleading indicators of its importance in everyday life. Self-esteem crops up everywhere, in part, simply because conceptual entrepreneurs are busy selling the word in books, magazines, and on television.

Selling is, after all, the business of conceptual entrepreneurs. It is their job, having discovered the key to happiness and success, to convince publishers and editors that it can sell books and magazines.

The frequent use of the word on television talk shows should likewise come as no surprise and should not be taken more seriously than it merits. The talk show genre pioneered by people such as Phil Donahue, Oprah Winfrey, and Geraldo Rivera, and extended by an increasingly sleazy array of competitors, is precisely where one might expect self-esteem to make frequent appearances. The television talk show is a place where individuals are encouraged to reveal the most intimate details of their lives in public and often vie with one another to seem the most outrageous and disreputable. Indeed, bookers for "trash TV" shows seek guests who can be counted on to provide audience-rousing performances. Not surprisingly, then, it is a context that attracts the most narcissistic types of people and licenses them to put themselves on display.

There can be no doubting the audience appeal of these programs, which in some ways resemble the circus freak shows that were widely popular a few decades ago. People went to freak shows to see bearded ladies and two-headed children, just as they now watch televised performances by people who inform their partners, on the air, that they have slept with their partner's best friend (or parent, sibling, child, etc.) and claim they did it because the partner's behavior lowered their self-esteem. Clearly these shows appeal to their audiences, given their high ratings. But why? Is it necessarily or even probably because the audience members identify with the freaks, engage in similar forms of conduct themselves, or display similar deformities?

Probably not. The appeal of freak shows (of the circus or the trash TV variety) may instead lie in the fact that they enable the audience to make moral distinctions between themselves and those whose behavior or talk they witness. The social function of freak shows of all kinds is in part to draw normative or moral boundaries—to make clear the differences between good and bad, right and wrong, normal and abnormal. Attention has shifted from the bizarre physical abnormalities of the circus freak show to the behavioral and psychological oddities put on view on the television talk show. But in both forms of the freak show, the audience is presented with the abnormal and can reassure itself of its own normality. Indeed, the contemporary talk show is a participatory event in which audience members can show their disagreement and disgust with guests, vent their moral spleens, and even put on their own narcissistic displays. Trash TV provides audiences with displays of behavior they love to hate.

Talk of self-esteem in such public places, then, may have an effect that is nearly the opposite of what critics fear. We should not suppose that those who hear talk of self-esteem automatically identify with it or become sym-

pathetic with those who use it. Instead, it may well be that they find it inappropriate, regard it as an indication that something is morally wrong with
those who use it, or find in this talk a way of reassuring themselves that they
have the appropriate kinds of personal experiences and moral commitments. A viewer who hears a mother on a talk show explain that she beat
her children because she had low self-esteem, which she claims was a result
of having been beaten herself, does not, then, necessarily adopt the language of self-esteem or identify with the abuser's perspective. Without
denying that low self-esteem might be a result of abuse, the viewer could
just as easily take the view that the abuser too readily offers self-esteem as an
excuse. In responding this way, the viewer in essence claims the moral high
ground, arguing that people are responsible for their behavior and should
not be so easily excused for their failings.

We must also make a crucial distinction between self-esteem as a word
commonly used in public discourse and as a label individuals attach to
themselves privately or in intimate settings. Almost all of the meanings of
self-esteem we have examined lie in the former realm rather than the latter.
That is, I have examined—and critics have examined—the meanings of self-
esteem largely as they appear in print and on television, in places where
people write or speak for public consumption. We cannot assume that
people use the word as frequently in private as in public, nor that even if they
do that the word has the same meanings in the one context as in the other.

Public discourse about self-esteem is a form of social theorizing. That
is, when writers describe the steps we can take to improve self-esteem they
are not only offering practical guidance for our lives but also telling us what
they think about the society and our relationships with it and with one
another. The author who offers ways of rethinking our evaluations of ourselves and thus restoring self-esteem through cognitive therapy is also
doing social theory. The implicit—and sometimes explicit—social theory is
that the social circumstances in which we live are complex, and we may not
be able to do much about them. The social theory in effect tells us to ignore
society and concentrate on the personal. Contrary to the message of, say,
feminists, that "the personal is political," the message of this form of self-
esteem advice is that "the personal is personal."

People can respond to this theoretical message in a variety of ways.
Some agree to it readily because it reinforces the message of individualism
that they have already received from their culture and from many other
sources. To offer people a method for thinking better of themselves is to urge
upon them the view that it is the individual's opinions that really count,
that one should not pay too much attention to what other people say or to
what one imagines they think. Other members of the audience perhaps
ignore the theoretical message because they are interested in remedies for
their personal pain and not in political ideas. Still others actively resist the

message, taking the explicit political stance that such confounding of personal troubles and public issues interferes with needed social changes.

Indeed, much of the criticism of the self-esteem movement and the self-help movement generally reflects this concern. In her study of the recovery movement, Elayne Rapping takes it and the self-esteem movement to task for what she calls the "diseasing of politics." These movements have, in her view, infiltrated feminism and undermined its quest for social change. The social conditions that damage the self-esteem of women, in her view, cannot be attacked by focusing on the individual experiences of women or by restoring them to psychic health. By slipping into such an individualistic focus, she argues, feminism and other change movements reduce their own effectiveness.[5] Author Wendy Kaminer's popular book, *I'm Dysfunctional, You're Dysfunctional,* adopts a very similar tone.[6] Self-help is bad for politics, in her view, and probably equally bad for personal development.

Public discourse about self-esteem is not the same thing as the private use of the word to label the feelings people have about themselves. The former serves the particular needs or purposes of a variety of actors on the public stage: conceptual entrepreneurs wishing to sell a product, political commentators, social critics, and social movement leaders who find in self-esteem ammunition for their own purposes, or teachers wishing to improve the lives of their students. Public discourse of this kind provides explanations, stimulates lines of social or political action, and provides support for other political or social ideologies. The latter—the private use of self-esteem as a label for feelings—serves the needs of individuals as they seek to interpret their own lives. We cannot predict the latter from the former—that is, the meanings that emerge in public discourse about self-esteem do not necessarily shape the private uses of the word.

Unfortunately, we do not know very much about how individuals actually use the word self-esteem to make sense of their own experiences. The social scientists who study self-esteem regard it as an attribute or characteristic of individuals that lends itself to empirical research. They seek to examine the sources and consequences of high or low self-esteem. But in doing so they take for granted that self-esteem exists as an individual characteristic, and from their vantage point how the individual labels his or her feelings is not highly relevant. From the standpoint of even such a sophisticated social scientist as the late Morris Rosenberg, people *have* self-concepts or self-esteem and the object is to measure these attributes. If, however, we think of self-esteem in the way I have proposed here, it is not an attribute of individuals but rather a way they may understand themselves. We do not know much about that, of course, because social scientists have not studied self-esteem in that way.

In the remaining pages of this book, I will explore the implications of viewing self-esteem as an interpretation of mood. Here, I believe, is where a key part of the reality of self-esteem lies. The claims of proponents and opponents of the myth of self-esteem by themselves tell us little either about individual experience or about the conditions under which contemporary people experience themselves. But by refocusing our understanding of self-esteem and treating it as interpreted mood, we can gain a better understanding of contemporary experience and of the reasons this term has proved so appealing.

SELF-ESTEEM AND THE MEDICALIZATION OF THE SELF

For the last century or so, the nature of the person has increasingly been subject to definition by scientists and experts. The invention of psychology and psychiatry established a beachhead for science in the territories of the mind, and their control over this territory has steadily increased. The development of humanistic psychology in the 1940s, exemplified by the client-centered approach of Carl Rogers, furthered this development. Even though Rogers departed from the scientific psychology of his day by making individual subjectivity central to his work, the nature of the person was still a matter held to lie within the province of the psychologist. Indeed, even religious positive thinkers such as Norman Vincent Peale turned to psychology for some of their ideas, signaling the decline of religion's ownership of this aspect of human experience.

In the last fifty years—roughly since the end of World War II—psychology in one form or another has become a major presence in our culture. It has spawned dozens of therapeutic systems and approaches, ranging from the scientifically and academically respectable to the bizarre. At one end of the spectrum, university psychology departments run training programs in clinical psychology, whose graduates must meet state licensing standards and who practice both in private offices and in various treatment facilities. At the other end of the spectrum, there is now a vast array of popular therapeutic methods, not taught within universities but rather in "institutes" and "schools" that are essentially entrepreneurial in nature.

All one need do to grasp the contemporary significance of this array of scientific and popular therapies is to consult the telephone book, which in my community contains about three pages of listings for psychologists, psychotherapists, and psychiatrists. These specialists practice in a small city with a small college and a nearby large town with a large university, with a total population of about 75,000. Academic places probably attract more than their share of people who think they need therapy and specialists who are eager to provide it. Even so, people in my vicinity can find a therapist almost more readily than they can find, say, a plumber or someone to repave the driveway. The area is likewise rich in alternative therapies.

During the same fifty years, medicine also made claims as a definer of human beings and their essential natures. Not only did medicine prove able to cure diseases and restore physical health, but increasingly it also claimed, through psychiatry, to hold the key to mental health. Orthodox Freudian psychoanalysis has given way to more diverse forms of therapy, and in recent years psychiatrists have turned increasingly to drugs in the treatment of mental illness. Although the basis of its claims has thus changed, organized medicine has nonetheless staked out the self, or what we call the self, as part of its territory.

The *Diagnostic and Statistical Manual,* on which mental health practitioners rely for the diagnosis and classification of mental illnesses, lists a bewildering array of forms of mental illness. More important, it brings under the rubric of illness many forms of behavior and problems of personal adjustment that once would have been viewed as problems of character or morality. The abuse of alcohol and other drugs, at one time thought to be forms of behavior that individuals could choose to abandon, now are regarded as treatable illnesses. Where once individuals were thought to be disagreeable or lacking in character, their behavior now is regarded as symptomatic of such illnesses as "narcissistic personality disorder" or "borderline personality disorder." Mental health practitioners have an arsenal of drugs and therapeutic techniques with which to treat these illnesses.

As the nature and problems of the person have fallen under the influence of this array of psychological and medical experts (or those who pretend to be experts) the self has become increasingly medicalized. The definition of a desirable or good self has not only gradually come to be shaped by these experts, but it has come to be seen in terms of health and illness. Behavior, once under the control of religion, law, and custom, has increasingly come under the control of one or another form of medicine. The person who was once thought to be capable of making rational choices, based upon adherence to social requirements, is now sometimes thought as powerless to overcome various infirmities of the mind and psyche without medical assistance. And the self—the culturally created center of the person's essential being—is increasingly measured by criteria of health and illness. The good self, the desirable self, is coming to be the healthy self.

Where does self-esteem fit into this process of medicalization? Put most simply, I think both public and private uses of the word self-esteem are moving in a medical direction. Increasingly, I suspect, high self-esteem is becoming thought of as an indicator of psychological or mental health, and low self-esteem as a form of illness. Public discourse about self-esteem still touches a great many different cultural nerves, and by no means have its medical connotations come to dominate its use. In fact, given the current level of criticism of the self-esteem movement, I suspect we will see a diminution of public discourse using the word rather than a drastic transformation in that realm. But I also think that where public discourse about self-esteem persists, especially in private contexts, it will increasingly take a medical, health-related turn.

The best evidence that such a turn is underway comes from the apparently growing association between self-esteem and various forms of mental illness, particularly major depression. By a growing association, I do not mean that people diagnosed as depressed are also becoming more likely to have self-esteem problems. Self-esteem has long been associated with depression, and in fact the *DSM* defines low self-esteem as one of the key symptoms of major depression. Instead, I mean that professionals and the public alike are increasingly thinking of low self-esteem as a treatable illness, and thinking of it in much the same way they think of depression.

It is significant that self-esteem—which I have argued is interpreted mood—should be associated with depression, which is defined in broad terms as a "disorder of mood." High self-esteem is not becoming equivalent to mental health in general nor is low self-esteem to mental illness in general, for there are far too many ways in which mental functioning can become disordered for that to occur. But self-esteem is clearly becoming associated—in terms of conception, treatment, and public perception—with various mood disorders, including anxiety and major depression.

One form of evidence indicative of this growing conceptual association between self-esteem and depression is the use of similar forms of treatment for each condition. Significantly, both are being treated by psychiatrists and other physicians, not only with "talking therapies" but also with psychoactive drugs. The version of psychotherapy that is most successful in the treatment of depression—cognitive therapy—is also now used in the treatment of low self-esteem. Indeed, the most popular self-esteem book now on the market guides readers through the very same therapeutic strategies used to treat depression. The antidepressive drugs that have come to dominate the treatment of depression—including the well-known Prozac and similar drugs—also appear to have the effect of raising self-esteem. A brief examination of these treatments will make clear how far the medicalization of self-esteem has come—and also why I think it is useful to conceive of self-esteem as interpreted mood.

Ten Days to Self-Esteem, by psychiatrist David D. Burns, is a large, workbook-style publication with a picture of the smiling doctor on the cover, along with a bright gold sticker advising the potential buyer that the method has been "Pioneered and Tested at the Presbyterian Medical Center of Philadelphia."[7] "In ten exciting steps," the cover advertises, "you will learn how to defeat depression, develop self-esteem, discover the secrets of joy in daily living." Burns also wrote *Feeling Good: The New Mood Therapy*, which is billed as a "breakthrough two and a half million best-seller" aimed at helping people with depression. Inside *Ten Days*, one learns that the book uses the method of cognitive therapy, which has proven to be as effective, if not more effective, the author says, than the use of antidepressant drugs in treating depression.

Ten Days to Self-Esteem is something of a marvel of medical technology—it is the latest in "bibliotherapy," as the author calls it. The book is chock-full of various tests that are to be taken by the reader as benchmarks in his or her progress in the treatment of low self-esteem. There is the Burns Anxiety Inventory, the Burns Depression Checklist, a Cost-Benefit Analysis on which the patient is to "list the advantages and disadvantages of a negative thought, feeling, or belief," a Daily Mood Log, and a Relationship Satisfaction Scale. There are multiple copies of these forms, since some of the scales are to be taken before and after each step. The steps themselves consist of exercises in which the reader becomes more aware of negative thoughts, analyzes them, finds new ways of describing the thoughts that makes him or her feel better, and thereby gradually reorients thinking from negative to positive. On the whole, the method is much like the approach of McKay and Fanning, which we considered in Chapter 3. A principal difference, however, is that *Ten Days* walks the reader through the steps one by one, inserting the proper form or exercise at each step along the way. One might just as well be following an exercise plan or filling out entries in a food diary in order to lose weight.

Throughout his book, Dr. Burns repeatedly associates self-esteem and depression. In places, I found myself forgetting the book's focus on self-esteem, partly because the word depression so frequently appears, as do the methods used successfully to measure and treat depression. The confounding of depression and self-esteem also reflects the fact that both are indeed grounded in mood, and seems to be, above all, the reader's mood that the author wishes to improve. "Feeling good feels wonderful," the back cover exclaims! "You owe it to yourself to feel good."

Depression is also treated by an arsenal of antidepressant drugs, most visibly in recent years by drugs such as Prozac. Such drugs work at the level of neurotransmission in the brain, and although the way in which they operate is not fully known, in general they increase the supply and prolong the action of such neurotransmitters as serotonin, norepinephrine, and dopamine. These neurotransmitters are responsible for the passing of messages along chains of neurons, and serotonin in particular is associated with the regulation of mood. By slowing the rate at which the neurotransmitters are reabsorbed by the transmitting neuron or destroyed by enzymes that work in the synapse, antidepressants have a reregulating effect on neural transmission.

Prozac, which works specifically on serotonin, has a range of positive effects on mental functioning. It brightens or lifts the person's mood, lessening or removing the negative and cloudy thinking, as well as the fog of despair that afflicts people suffering from major depression. It can make people more socially outgoing, more energetic, and more capable of functioning in everyday life. It also has the capacity to reduce anxiety, and it is approved for the treatment of obsessive-compulsive disorder, a form of mental illness in which the person repeatedly and uncontrollably engages in such behavior as washing hands or checking the locks on doors.

Prozac also raises self-esteem. As Peter Kramer, the author of the best-selling book *Listening to Prozac,* has pointed out, patients who seek treatment for depression frequently suffer from low self-esteem.[8] As it brightens mood, Prozac also seems to raise self-esteem, not only for those with major depression but for those on the borderline of this illness whose symptoms do not quite meet the diagnostic criteria. Often this increased self-esteem has a rather swift onset—it does not occur gradually, but seemingly overnight. After the four weeks or so normally required for an antidepressant to take effect, some patients find their self-esteem rather markedly improved. They not only feel good, but they feel good about themselves.

It is not difficult to understand why Prozac has this effect, particularly if we think of self-esteem as an interpretation of mood. By helping individuals function better in relationships with others, antidepressants no doubt help them behave in ways that will earn them approval. But more fundamentally than that, Prozac directly brightens mood—it works precisely on the range of bodily feelings we have called mood, and in doing so it provides the individual with a new and desirable set of feelings to interpret. Given the availability of self-esteem as a label, and especially given the long-time clinical association of self-esteem with depression, it is not surprising that both patients and their physicians interpret these changes in terms of self-esteem.

The significance of antidepressants for the medicalization of the self lies partly in the fact that physicians can now claim specific expertise in raising low self-esteem. Just as the success of cognitive therapy adds to the arsenal of the psychologist (or the psychiatrist inclined to try talk therapies before medication), Prozac adds to the arsenal of the psychiatrist and the family practitioner. Moreover, as people seek treatment for anxiety or low self-esteem, these conditions become defined as specific illnesses treatable by specific methods. Just as physicians treat diabetes with insulin injections, they treat low self-esteem with Prozac. And just as no one doubts the efficacy of insulin or the reality of diabetes, few will entertain doubts about antidepressants and low self-esteem.

Psychologists who use cognitive therapy and psychiatrists who use Prozac are often at odds with one another about treatment methods. The former dislike the rapidity with which the latter turn to drug therapy; and the latter are often dissatisfied with the reluctance of the former to accept the biochemical foundations of depression or self-esteem. Psychologists and psychiatrists alike are sometimes criticized and perhaps more often ignored by the legions of alternative health practitioners who have their own methods for improving self-esteem.

But what they all have in common is a tendency to think of high self-esteem as an indicator of health. We should not find this surprising. In a culture that makes happiness (however defined) a chief goal of life, we should not be surprised to find that individual mood gains in significance or that the words we use to describe and interpret this mood take a medical turn. If happiness is our cultural prime directive, being in a good mood is one of the chief ways we come to know we are happy. If we are ready to spend hundreds of millions of dollars on fitness equipment as well as hundreds of millions more on the care of the body, it is not surprising that we also spend our dollars on improving our moods. And if we can find a word like self-esteem, which has the virtue of avoiding at least some of the negative connotations of mental illness and depression, so much the better.

If there is something real about self-esteem, then, it is in the capacity of this word to label universal human somatic and psychological responses to success and failure in culturally appropriate ways. It is the latest word for happiness in a culture where happiness is important. Self-esteem is important, as its proponents recognize, but not because it is something whose pursuit will bring happiness. It is important because many of those who achieve happiness will increasingly call it self-esteem and think of it as a sign of health and vigor. The pursuit of self-esteem is something to worry about, as the critics have argued, but not because it undermines traditional cultural values. If anything, the babble of discourse about self-esteem reaffirms our cultural values and debates, and the varying meanings the term has acquired signifies the vigor of the culture rather than its demise.

We should worry about the pursuit of self-esteem not because it will do harm, but because it will not do the good it promises. Psychic health, like physical health, is an unquestionable good, and it does not really matter what we call it. But neither form of health guarantees that people, individually or collectively, will do what they should do to remedy injustice, teach children skills that will help them lead productive and happy lives, or end the scourge of racism. Enhanced self-esteem is no more a shortcut to happiness or a better society than a low cholesterol count or well-defined abs. Healthy selves in healthy bodies can put their energies to good purposes or bad ones.

NOTES

1. For helpful analyses of this question by anthropologists, see Richard A. Schweder and Robert A. Levine, eds. *Culture Theory: Essays on Mind, Self, and Emotion* (New York: Cambridge University Press, 1984).

2. The sociological view of emotions is explored in John P. Hewitt, *Self and Society: A Symbolic Interactionist Social Psychology,* 7th ed. (Boston: Allyn and Bacon, 1997), Chapters 2 and 4.

3. David Riesman, with Nathan Glazer, and Ruel Denney, *The Lonely Crowd: A Study of the Changing American Character.* New Haven: Yale University Press, 1950.

4. Allen Wheelis, *The Quest for Identity.* New York: Norton, 1958; Orrin Klapp, *The Collective Search for Identity.* New York: Holt, Rinehart, Winston, 1969; Christopher Lasch, *The Culture of Narcissism.* New York: Basic Books, 1978; Lasch, *The Minimal Self: Psychic Survival in Troubled Times.* New York: Norton, 1984.

5. Elayne Rapping, *The Culture of Recovery.* Boston: Beacon Press, 1996.

6. Wendy Kaminer, *I'm Dysfunctional, You're Dysfunctional.* Reading, Mass.: Addison-Wesley, 1992.

7. David D. Burns, M. D., *Ten Days to Self-Esteem.* New York: Quill, 1993.

8. Peter Kramer, *Listening to Prozac.* New York: Viking, 1993, Chapter 7.

Further Reading

SOURCES AND CONSEQUENCES
OF SELF-ESTEEM

The scholarly literature on self-esteem is so vast that it is difficult to know where to begin surveying it. The following sources provide a variety of avenues for reading about the development of self-esteem and its personal and social consequences. All adopt a social scientific approach to the study of self-esteem, taking for granted that self-esteem exists and that it is an important human attribute.

Coopersmith, Stanley, *The Antecedents of Self-Esteem.* San Francisco: W. H. Freeman, 1967.

Gecas, Viktor, and Peter Burke, "Self and Identity," chapter two in Karen Cook, Gary Alan Fine, and James S. House, eds., *Sociological Perspectives on Social Psychology.* Boston: Allyn and Bacon, 1995.

Mecca, Andrew M., Neil J. Smelser, and John Vasconcellos, eds., *The Social Importance of Self-Esteem.* Berkeley: University of California Press, 1989.

Rosenberg, Morris, *Society and the Adolescent Self-Image.* Princeton: Princeton University Press, 1965.

Rosenberg, Morris, *Conceiving the Self.* New York: Basic Books, 1979.

Rosenberg, Morris, and Roberta G. Simmons, *Black and White Self-Esteem: The Urban School Child.* Washington, D. C.: American Sociological Association, 1972.

Wells, L. Edward, and Gerald Marwell, *Self-Esteem.* Beverly Hills: Sage, 1976.

Wylie, Ruth, *The Self-Concept: Theory and Research on Selected Topics.* Lincoln: University of Nebraska Press, 1979.

AMERICAN CHARACTER
AND CULTURE

Readers interested in exploring in greater detail the ways in which popular and social scientific discourse are linked to culture would do well to explore the literature of American culture and character. In my own work in this area (cited here), I have found a number of sources that help delineate the issues and contain important insights.

Bellah, Robert N., Richard Madsen, William M. Sullivan, Anne Swidler, and Steven M. Tipton, *Habits of the Heart: Individualism and Commitment in American Life.* Berkeley: University of California Press, 1985.

Burns, Rex, *Success in America: The Yeoman Dream and the Industrial Revolution.* Amherst: University of Massachusetts Press, 1976.

de Tocqueville, Alexis, *Democracy in America,* ed. Phillips Bradley. New York: Vintage, 1945.

Erikson, Kai T., *Everything in Its Path.* New York: Simon and Schuster, 1976.

Gans, Herbert, Nathan Glazer, Joseph R. Gusfield, and Christopher Jencks, eds., *On the Making of Americans: Essays in Honor of David Riesman.* Philadelphia: University of Pennsylvania Press, 1979.

Greven, Philip, *The Protestant Temperament: Patterns of Child Rearing, Religious Experience, and the Self in Early America.* New York: Knopf, 1977.

Hewitt, John P., *Dilemmas of the American Self.* Philadelphia: Temple University Press, 1989.

Howe, Irving, *The American Newness.* Cambridge: Harvard University Press, 1986.

Lasch, Christopher, *The Culture of Narcissism.* New York: Basic Books, 1978.

Lears, T. J. Jackson, *No Place of Grace: Antimodernism and the Transformation of American Culture, 1880–1920.* Chicago: University of Chicago Press, 1994.

Lewis, R. W. B., *The American Adam: Innocence, Tragedy, and Tradition in the Nineteenth Century.* Chicago: University of Chicago Press, 1955.

McClay, Wilfred M., *The Masterless: Self and Society in Modern America.* Chapel Hill: University of North Carolina Press, 1994.

Meyer, Donald, *The Positive Thinkers,* rev. ed. Middletown, Conn.: Wesleyan University Press, 1988.

Riesman, David, with Nathan Glazer, and Ruel Denney, *The Lonely Crowd: A Study of the Changing American Character.* New Haven: Yale University Press, 1950.

Saum, Lewis O., *The Popular Mood of Pre-Civil War America.* Westport, Conn.: Greenwood, 1980.

Varenne, Hervé, *Americans Together: Structured Diversity in a Midwestern Town.* New York: Teachers College Press, 1977.

Wright, Will, *Six Guns and Society: A Structural Study of the Western.* Berkeley: University of California Press, 1975.

THEORETICAL ORIENTATIONS

In this book I have sought to work from a symbolic interactionist (but also constructionist, and sometimes even postmodernist or poststructuralist) point of view, without making the theoretical approach intrusive, heavy-handed, or obscure. My ideas derive from far too many sources to permit a simple prescription for further reading in this area, but I have found the following publications especially helpful. My own symbolic interactionist exposition, cited here, contains other helpful suggestions.

Foucault, Michel, *History of Sexuality. Vol. 1: An Introduction.* London: Allen Lane, 1979.

Hewitt, John P., *Self and Society: A Symbolic Interactionist Social Psychology,* 7th ed. Boston: Allyn and Bacon, 1997.

Joas, Hans, *Pragmatism and Social Theory.* Chicago: University of Chicago Press, 1993.

Lukes, Steven, *Individualism.* New York: Harper, 1973.

Rose, Niklas, *Governing the Soul: The Shaping of the Private Self.* London: Routledge, 1990.

Schwartz, Theodore, Geoffrey M. White, and Catherine A. Lutz, eds., *New Directions in Psychological Anthropology.* New York: Cambridge University Press, 1992.

Schweder, Richard A., and Robert A. LeVine, eds., *Culture Theory: Essays on Mind, Self, and Emotion.* New York: Cambridge University Press, 1984.

Spector, Malcolm, and John I. Kitsuse, *Constructing Social Problems.* New York: Aldine de Gruyter, 1987.

Index